Starting on the Buddhist Path

An Invitation

Sagaraghosa Rosemary Tennison

Windhorse Publications
38 Newmarket Road
Cambridge CB5 8DT
info@windhorsepublications.com
windhorsepublications.com

Cover design by Katarzyna Manecka
Text design by Francesca Romano Design
Typesetting and layout by Tarajyoti
Cover image and illustrations by Padmacandra, © Padmacandra, 2023
Photographs by Jeremy Peters, © Jeremy Peters, 2023
Printed by Bell & Bain Ltd, Glasgow

British Library Cataloguing in Publication Data:
A catalogue record for this book is available from the British Library.

ISBN 978-1-915342-08-9

Praise for *Starting on the Buddhist Path: An Invitation*

Sagaraghosa writes with the tone of a trusted friend, sharing wisdom and perspective with a guiding grace. The book provides a safe space for readers to investigate and reflect on the delicate intricacies of developing their Buddhist practice. – **Sharon Salzberg**, author of *Lovingkindness* and *Real Life*

In *Starting on the Buddhist Path*, Sagaraghosa is inviting us to see and experience for ourselves the jewel that is Buddhism. Her writing is simple and evocative, and at the same time radiant with the wisdom of the Buddhist tradition. She shows us so many different glittering facets of this precious jewel – the Buddha, his teachings, the spiritual community, the historical development of Buddhism, iconography and ritual, the wisdom teachings that help us to gain Enlightenment ourselves. Full of examples, poems, and stories, ancient and new, this wonderful book is recommended for anyone, young or old, interested in travelling the Buddhist path to freedom. – **Vajrashura**, Buddhist teacher in the Triratna Buddhist Community

Starting on the Buddhist Path takes you by the hand – especially if you're new to Buddhism – and guides you, with great care and thoughtfulness, through Buddhist teachings and practices. As well as telling you what Buddhism says, it will help you explore *why* its teachings could be important for you – right now and in your life as a whole. – **Vishvapani Blomfield**, author of *Gautama Buddha: The Life and Teachings of the Awakened One*

For Katie and Max

Contents

About the Author

Sagaraghosa Rosemary Tennison spent much of her working life commissioning mathematics books for schools at Cambridge University Press. She started meditating in 1996. On ordination into the Triratna Buddhist Order in 2005, she was given the name Sagaraghosa, which means 'she whose voice is like the ocean.' After ordination she led courses in meditation and Buddhism for newcomers for fourteen years, and also led study on a wide variety of Buddhist topics, both at the Cambridge Buddhist Centre. Sangharakshita, the founder of the Triratna Buddhist Community, appointed her as one of his literary executors.

She delights in making the teachings of the Buddha accessible to as many people as possible and thereby changing their lives for the better. To do this, she uses imaginative approaches and she encourages people to try things out and to reflect on their experience.

She has been married for more than fifty years to a patient and supportive (non-Buddhist) husband, and has two delightful adult daughters and two much-loved grandchildren.

Publisher's Acknowledgements

Windhorse Publications wish to gratefully acknowledge a grant from the Future Dharma Fund and the Triratna European Chairs' Assembly Fund towards the production of this book.

We also wish to acknowledge and thank the individual donors who gave to the book's production via our 'Sponsor-a-book' campaign.

Audio Recordings

Starting on the Buddhist Path has been produced with some accompanying guided meditations by Sagaraghosa, and can be streamed directly from the web.

Please go to: https://tinyurl.com/SotBP-audio

Introduction

This is the book I wish I'd had when I started to become interested in Buddhism. It has been written for those who know that they would like to explore Buddhism and for those who just want to find out more about it. The book is based on my fourteen years of experience of teaching an 'Introduction to Buddhism' course at the Cambridge Buddhist Centre in the UK, and the study and reflection I did over that time and have continued to do since.

In the current world, there is much suffering. This book is my gift to the future, with a hope that it can help to give rise to awareness, kindness, and joy for you and for those you come into contact with.

There are three aspects to the Buddhist path: ethics, meditation, and wisdom. Meditation is extremely important, and the Buddhism course mentioned above was taught alongside meditation. However, this book does not teach you to meditate, because it is hard to learn meditation from a book, and there are plenty of books and apps already available that teach meditation. By contrast, there is relatively little available that gives an easy overview of the teachings of the Buddha. So this book focuses on ethics and wisdom. However, your understanding will be greatly enhanced if you also meditate. There are some suggestions for resources in the last chapter, and there are a couple of guided meditations within the book to give a flavour of what you can expect from meditation.

The only way you can truly come to understand the Buddha's teaching is by exploring it in your own experience. So the book is full of practices, reflections, and things to do. Practices will be useful if you do them more than once, ideally regularly, because they can make a positive difference to your mind. Reflections are an opportunity to pause in your reading and think about how the teachings might apply to you. Activities are opportunities to explore what happens when you do something specific. In an ideal world, you would be able to discuss what you find with someone else, but these explorations will be helpful even if that is not possible for you.

The first six chapters cover the content of the 'Introduction to Buddhism' course that I used to lead. Chapter 7 provides an opportunity to go deeper and to gain more insight into how we operate as human beings. It encourages a gentle exploration into the topic of non-self. An understanding of this topic has the potential to take wisdom to a deeper level.

Chapter 8 provides some suggestions to take the practice of Buddhism further, by meditating, going on retreat, and reading more widely. It also points to some online resources.

There are many people who have contributed to this book. Foremost is my wise friend Ruchiraketu, who devised and taught the course that this book is based on. I learned a lot from supporting the course that he taught before teaching it myself. He has also given me some helpful advice about specific content. Most importantly, for more than twenty years he has provided wise guidance for my exploration of the Buddhist path.

In addition, I would like to thank Dhammamegha at Windhorse Publications for encouraging me to write, providing helpful feedback, and overseeing the process of producing the whole book. She has been helpful with her suggestions and effective in managing the project. Many people have given helpful comments, and I would particularly like to thank Dhivan for so many helpful corrections and suggestions of alternative approaches. The book has been transformed by their suggestions.

Two friends have particularly helped with the illustrations: Padmacandra has produced the delightful drawings, and Jeremy Peters has provided beautiful photographs. In addition,

Saddharaja produced the picture of the wheel of life. Good illustrations transform a book, and I'm most grateful to all of them.

Dhatvisvari has provided skilful editing. Michelle at Windhorse Publications has overseen production with enthusiasm, and Walter and others at the publishers have dealt with the marketing and administration that are essential to the success of any publication.

Many other friends have contributed to the ideas in the book. When I've felt stuck, I've taken the opportunity to discuss ideas with whoever I've been with, and the result has inevitably been a stimulating conversation. My daughter Vimaladipa has been particularly helpful by listening, encouraging, and asking pertinent questions. Too many other people have been involved for me to list you all, but you know who you are.

Lastly, but by no means least, I would like to express my gratitude to my husband, Barry. He has encouraged me to write and has been the first person to read each chapter in turn. His feedback has been invaluable in helping to make the writing accessible. I'm touched by the way that he has confidence in me and appreciates what I do, even though he does not identify as a Buddhist himself.

1 The Why, What, and How of Following the Buddhist Path

Why have you started to read this book? There are many reasons why you may have decided that it is worth exploring Buddhism. For me, it was partly the hope that I might become less overwhelmed by my emotions, because I wanted the wisdom to make a positive difference to the world, and I was interested to explore new ideas. For many people, it is to experience more peace and less stress. For one of my friends, it was wanting to explore altered states of consciousness and because Buddhism provided an alternative to our materialistic culture: a way that involved mystery and depth, but avoided some of the problems of Christianity. One of these reasons may resonate with you, or your motivation may be completely different. Whatever the reason, I hope that this book will be helpful.

Why explore Buddhism?

For fourteen years, I taught introductory courses in Buddhism and meditation, and, when the people I taught reached the end of their courses, they would often be surprised at the benefits. These could include improved relationships, as well as the more expected lessening of stress. It has been very moving to meet people who finished courses several years ago, and who come up and thank me for the way it changed their lives. The changes can include feeling more joyful, or having more positive relationships, or feeling more confident.

Such people always impress me, as changes like this require an effort. Although hearing about the ideas and practices of Buddhism can be helpful, it is the effort of regular practice and reflecting on the ideas that really makes a substantial difference possible. So this book is an invitation to explore and to discover the positive changes that are possible for you. We shall start by exploring what Buddhism is and how it is best to approach it.

What is Buddhism?

Rather than being a system of beliefs, Buddhism is a path of personal and social transformation, a path that leads to more contentment and equanimity for ourselves, more connection between people, and a bigger and more realistic perspective on society. To follow this path, we need to be active in the way we engage. So in this book you will find that there are times when I'll suggest that you stop and do something. It may be that you are invited to listen to a meditation or reflect on a question; it may be that you are invited to write down some thoughts or ideas; it may be that you are invited to take an action in your everyday life and to notice the consequences. It is important not to skip over these invitations. They are opportunities to learn and to make positive differences in your life, and they are the main way in which you will be able to benefit from your exploration of Buddhism.

Let's start by taking a broad perspective on what we are bringing to this exploration. First, there is our context: what we bring from our culture and the views and attitudes that we already have. In societies where Buddhism is, or was, the dominant religion, people were more likely to accept the teachings on faith or religious authority. However, you may want to ask questions such as:

- When did the Buddha live? Do we even know that he existed? (a historical perspective)
- Where did the Buddhist religion develop and what was its context? (a geographical perspective)
- What reasons are there for accepting or following these teachings? (a critical perspective)

More helpfully, we can also ask questions such as:

- Is this teaching true in my experience?
- What happens when I try out this practice with an open mind?

Some of us can be sceptical about anything we can't easily understand rationally or can't explain in words. You might find that this affects your response to some of the ideas. For example, you may be inclined to ignore traditional stories that involve supernatural beings or don't fit modern scientific ideas. If so, I would encourage you to be as open as you can, and try out even things that raise doubts in you.

When we explore something, we inevitably bring our habits of thought and perception. One of the most exciting and engaging aspects of Buddhism is that it changes *how* we see the world, and questions these habits. You will learn to look *with* a Buddhist viewpoint, and not just *at* that viewpoint. So understanding Buddhism is not just about examining Buddhist views: it is about exploring and developing your ways of viewing.

There are four different aspects of Buddhism that we shall explore. Together they enable us to explore Buddhism in its fullness.

- **Concepts, teachings, ideas**, basically, the teachings of the Buddha, such as the four noble truths, the eightfold path, non-self. These are the teachings that we shall start to explore in chapter 3. Chapter 7 takes the teachings deeper.
- **Attitudes**, for example, non-violence, kindness, interest. The approach we take is as important as the content. So there can be challenges in learning from a book, rather than from a person who embodies these attitudes.
- **Practices**, for example, meditation, mindfulness, generosity, ethics, ritual. These appear throughout the book, and particularly in chapters 4 and 6.
- **Symbols, images, metaphors, stories**, for example, the three jewels, the lotus, the mandala. The meaning of these symbols will become clearer as we progress through the book, and will be explored particularly in chapter 6.

Reflection
What is motivating you to explore the Buddhist path?

What context do you come from? For example, do you have a scientific training? Are you interested in the mystical aspects of Buddhism? What else in your background is likely to colour the way in which you approach Buddhism?

During your life, you will already have changed your view of the world. What we think is important as adults is different from what we thought when we were children. For example, your relationship with toys will most likely have changed, and maybe you're more aware that other people have emotions just like you do. Write down some ways in which your view of the world has changed during your life.

Practice: awareness meditation (ten minutes)

We have done quite a lot of thinking and taking in concepts, so let's do some practice. Below is a summary of how to do the practice, and you can find a led version here: https://tinyurl.com/SotBP-audio.

- First, sitting comfortably in a way that is dignified and relaxed.
- Looking around the room, you can choose what objects to attend to. Attend in particular to colours.
- Now noticing shapes and lines. What do you notice about the colours when you do that?
- Now choosing to listen. What then happens to the shapes and colours? Listening to sounds far and near for a minute or two, you may want to close your eyes.
- Now bringing awareness to physical sensations: temperature, touch, contact with what you are sitting on, sensations in the body, joints, and muscles.

- Bringing a gentle, kindly awareness into the feet and then into the hands. Noticing, in particular, any touch sensations, or tingling.
- If the mind wanders, congratulating yourself for noticing and gently bringing more awareness to the sensations in the body again.
- Settling attention on the sensations of breathing – perhaps having a couple of deliberate deeper breaths so that the sensations are more obvious before returning to breathing naturally. Perhaps bringing awareness to the abdomen rising and falling or to the ribs expanding as you breathe in and releasing as you breathe out. Doing this for a couple of minutes.
- Broadening awareness to your whole body sitting in the room.
- Bringing attention back to the room.

This practice shows how you are able to direct attention to your surroundings and to the body. You may have found that distracting thoughts kept arising. This is normal, and you should congratulate yourself for noticing that this is happening. The mind is often called a 'monkey mind' in Buddhist texts, as it's like a monkey going from branch to branch in a tree, never settling in one place for long.

Instead, you may have found some unexpected calm or stillness. In that case, the danger is that you may be disappointed when your experience is different next time you try to meditate. As best you can, simply take an interest in whatever arises, without holding on to what is pleasant or pushing away what is unpleasant.

How to engage with Buddhism

There are three things that we all need in order to change and grow:

1. an ideal or direction in which to go;
2. practices to do that will take us in that direction;
3. and the support of others to encourage and guide us.

In Buddhism, we have what are called 'three jewels' that serve this function. The word 'jewels' is a metaphor that indicates that these are precious.

The first jewel is golden and is the Buddha, who is the symbol of Enlightenment, particularly as embodied in Siddhartha Gautama, the person who discovered the path to human perfection. He provides our ideal. We shall explore this jewel in detail in chapter 2.

The second jewel is blue and is the Dharma, the symbol of the path, the host of insights and practical guidelines the Buddha taught that help us to plot a path towards Enlightenment.

An image for the Dharma is a wheel. When the Buddha gave his first sermon, it is said that he set the wheel of the Dharma in motion. The turning of the wheel symbolizes the great change that provides the possibility of Enlightenment for us all. We shall mainly explore this jewel in chapters 3 and 4.

The third jewel is red and symbolizes the Sangha. 'Sangha' means 'spiritual community', and is the company of those who are also on this quest for Enlightenment, as well as the teachers of the past and present from whom we can learn.

Soon after his Enlightenment, it is said that the Buddha had a vision of a lotus pond with some lotuses as buds, and some standing well above the water ready to flower. In the same way, he saw that there were some people who were capable of understanding the Dharma easily, and others who might take a little longer to flower. So he realized that it was worth the effort of teaching. We can imagine a group of lotuses as a symbol of the spiritual community. We shall explore this jewel in chapter 5.

You must already be motivated to want to know more about Buddhism because you have started reading this book, so you already have some sense of the direction you want to go in. Something I have found fascinating is how that ideal can change. When I started learning about Buddhism, I was in a stressful job; I experienced a lot of anxiety, and could be overwhelmed with obsessional thoughts about my success or failure and what other people thought of me. So part of the direction of travel that interested me was to go towards equanimity, which to me meant not feeling things so deeply. However, as I have practised and developed some equanimity, it has become clear that equanimity is not what I imagined when I began: the emotions are sometimes still there, but what has changed is that they don't bother me so much. It is like riding a wave rather than expecting that the waves would no longer be there. This is a big change from being bowled over by them, which was where I started from.

That early vision was helpful in motivating me to discover more and to practise, even though it was later modified. When you follow the Buddhist path, there are some surprising twists and turns, and that is one thing that makes it so interesting.

Reflection (for about ten minutes)

You probably have some sense of the direction you want to go in, even if it is difficult to access. Here is a reflection that might help you explore what that direction might be in more detail.

Start by sitting as comfortably as you can, and bringing awareness to how your body is supported by the ground and the chair. Notice particularly the sensations in the feet.

For the first reflection, as best you can, bring to mind a moment that felt more than usually positive or meaningful for you - perhaps you felt contented, in tune with the world, more fully alive and energetic. It might be a time when you were out in nature, or a time when you felt a warm connection with others, or something else entirely.

- Remember the place, what you could see, any sounds, any smells.
- Remember how you were feeling and any thoughts or lack of thoughts.

If you were to live on the basis of that:

- What would you say was important?
- What would be your attitude towards life and other people?
- What would seem important to do?
- Is there any symbol or image that might help you remember?
- Are there any differences from the way you normally live?

What the Buddha said about his teachings

In what follows, I give five examples of what the Buddha said about his teachings. In each case, I have simplified the texts slightly so that the stories will be more comprehensible. Each example has a lesson that will be helpful when you read the rest of the book and try out the reflections, activities, and practices.

The importance of awareness

The first example illustrates how awareness is an important aspect of Buddhist practice. Noticing what is happening can be an important first step, as it makes us aware of the place we are starting from.

One time, a man asked the Buddha what happened when householders followed his teaching. Among other things, the Buddha said this:

> [A householder] becomes one who acts in full awareness when going forward and returning; who acts in full awareness when looking ahead and looking away; who acts in full awareness when flexing and extending their limbs; who acts in full awareness when wearing their robes and carrying their outer robe and bowl; who acts in full awareness when eating, drinking, consuming food, and tasting; who acts in full awareness when defecating and urinating; who acts in full awareness when walking, standing, sitting, falling asleep, waking up, talking, and keeping silent.[1]

So Buddhist practice isn't necessarily about doing something different, but instead about doing differently what we normally do and becoming more aware of what we are doing. The lesson we can take from this is that *how* we act is important as well as *what* we do. Even simple everyday tasks can become part of Buddhist practice if we do them with awareness and kindness. One Buddhist teacher said that it is possible to become enlightened while doing the ironing. When I was working, I used to make a practice of being aware of my movements when fetching a drink of tea or coffee during the day.

The simile of the arrow: questions the Buddha wouldn't answer

We can look to a religious leader to provide an explanation of the world. However, the Buddha was focused on reducing suffering for ourselves and others. Some of the Buddha's followers wanted him to answer metaphysical questions. In one of the early Buddhist texts, a monk is explicit about this and asks the following questions:

- Is the world eternal or not eternal?
- Is the world finite or infinite?
- Is the life principle the same as the body or different from it?
- Does the Buddha exist after death, not exist after death, both exist and not exist after death, or neither exist nor not exist after death?

These questions reflect the time and culture in which the Buddha lived. We might have questions such as:

- Is there life after death?
- Is the universe eternal or not eternal?
- Is there life on other planets?
- Is there just one universe or are there many?

> The Buddha said: 'It is as if there were a man struck by an arrow that was smeared thickly with poison; his friends and companions, his family and relatives would summon a doctor to see the arrow. And the man might say, "I will not draw out this arrow as long as I do not know the caste of the man by whom I was struck, his name and his family, whether he was tall or short or medium height." That man would not discover these things, but that man would die.'[2]

This story shows that we can't expect the Buddha to answer abstract questions. Instead, he was interested in how human beings function and in helping us transcend suffering. Because of this, the Buddha is traditionally thought of as being like a physician who heals people of their suffering. So we can expect to learn what it might be helpful to do when life is difficult, rather than why we are experiencing what we are experiencing. Buddhist teachings are very practical.

The blind man and the elephant

Next we come to a story told by the Buddha that illustrates how our interpretation of something depends on what we are focusing on. There are many examples in the political sphere, but I've noticed it on a much more mundane level with dandelions. The dandelion flower looks very beautiful when I simply observe it, but I've also noticed times when I want to dig up the plant in flower when it has taken root in my garden and is obscuring the flowers I have planted.

At one time, many people were quarrelling about the meaning of the Dharma, so the Buddha told a story. He said that in past times there was a king who asked for all those blind from birth to be brought together and to be shown an elephant.

To some he presented the head of the elephant, saying, 'This is an elephant.' To some he presented an ear of the elephant, saying, 'This is an elephant.' To some he presented a tusk, to some the trunk, to some the body, to some the foot, to some the hindquarters, to some the tail, to some the tuft at the end of the tail, saying, 'This is an elephant.'

> Then the king asked the blind people what the elephant was like, and they each gave a different answer, saying, 'An elephant is like this, an elephant is not like that! An elephant is not like this, an elephant is like that!' They fought each other with their fists. And the king was delighted with the spectacle.[3]

This image illustrates how our views of things depend on where and how we are looking. Buddhism is vast, and is practised differently by different people. A practice that is helpful for people in one country or time may not be so helpful for people in a different country or at a different time. For example, people nowadays can be very self-critical, whereas people in the Buddha's time in India didn't seem to have that problem. Even people in the same time and country have different tendencies. The lesson here is that we need to try out any recommendations in our own experience to find out how helpful they are for us. Also it's good to remember that what helps us may not help someone else – it might not even help us on a different day!

The elephant's footprint

Now we come to an analogy for how to approach the Buddhist path. With the Buddhist path, we are trying to find Enlightenment, and this is compared to a woodsman trying to find a big bull elephant.

The Buddha told the story of a wise woodsman who entered an elephant wood and saw a big elephant's footprint. The woodsman did not conclude that the footprint was from a big bull elephant, as some small she-elephants leave big footprints. He followed the footprints, and saw some scrapings high up. He still did not conclude that this came from a big bull elephant, as there were some tall she-elephants with prominent teeth. He followed further and also saw marks made by tusks, but he still did not conclude that this came from a big bull elephant as there were some she-elephants with tusks. So he followed further, and saw broken branches and a bull elephant at the base of a tree. Then he concluded that this was a big bull elephant. So similarly, the Buddha said, it is only after practising for some time that a disciple can conclude that the Buddha is fully enlightened.[4]

The lesson from this story is that we can only be certain about Enlightenment once we have experienced it for ourselves. However, we can see promising signs along the way. So it is fine to have some scepticism about what the Buddha taught. However, that doesn't mean that we should ignore what he said. Instead, it is helpful to follow any promising footsteps and promising marks. If we do this, then we have a chance of eventually experiencing Enlightenment.

The bamboo acrobats

As a context for this story, it is helpful to know that in the Buddha's day there were acrobats who used to travel from village to village and perform in pairs. One of them would hold a bamboo pole, and the other would climb up it and perform some acrobatics.

[The Buddha addressed the monks:] Once upon a time there was a teacher of acrobats using a bamboo pole. He placed the pole straight up on his shoulder and told his disciple: 'While going up and down on the pole, you protect me and I will also protect you. Protecting each other we will put on a show and gain much wealth.'

Then the disciple of acrobatics said to the teacher of acrobatics: 'It won't do, as you said. Instead, we should each take care to protect ourselves. Then we will put on a show and gain much wealth. We will be physically at ease and yet I will get down safely.'

The teacher of acrobatics said: 'As you said, we will take care to protect ourselves, this is correct and is also the meaning of what I said.'

[The Buddha said:] 'Having protected oneself, one also protects the other; protecting the other and oneself is proper protection. How does one protect others by protecting oneself? By becoming familiar with one's own mind, developing it, protecting it accordingly, and attaining realization. How does one protect oneself by protecting others? By the gift of fearlessness, the gift of non-violation, the gift of harmlessness, by having a mind of benevolence and empathy for the other.'[5]

This story illustrates how our practice needs to involve both looking after ourselves and looking after others. We do this by cultivating both mindfulness and kindness. The disciple's response reminds me of the instruction on a plane that, if emergency oxygen masks are released, you should put on your own mask before helping others. Similarly, we need to be mindful of what we are experiencing and how that is affecting us before we can help others effectively.

Reflection

Does your motivation tend towards looking after yourself or towards looking after others? Find an example where looking after yourself helped with looking after someone else, and an example where looking after someone else helped with your own well-being.

The reflection illustrates a more general lesson from this story, namely the limitations that polarized alternatives or black-and-white thinking can create: in this case, *either* looking after ourselves *or* looking after others. It is more helpful to think in terms of *both* looking after ourselves *and* looking after others. There are many instances where it is helpful to move from black-and-white alternatives to something more inclusive.

Here is a summary of the main points of this chapter. We will return to some of them later in the book.

- Buddhism can bring many benefits if it is practised. It is about how people function and how they can change.
- For Buddhists, there are three jewels that are important: the Buddha, who provides an ideal we are moving towards; the Buddha's teachings, the Dharma, which provide a way to move towards that ideal; and the support and guidance of others who are also following the path, the sangha.
- *How* we act is important as well as *what* we do.
- The practices that are helpful vary according to the person and the context they are in, so a useful attitude is to try practices out with curiosity to find out whether they help you.
- Before we reach Enlightenment, we cannot be sure about the goal, so we need to follow promising signs and the path will become clearer and clearer as we do so.

- Where there seem to be alternatives, it can be helpful to change to an approach of both ... and .... In particular, we need to practise *both* helping ourselves *and* helping others, and that will involve both mindfulness and kindness.

2 The Buddha

The Buddha lived about 2,500 years ago in northern India. Much of the information about his life comes from stories that have been told over the years by his followers. Although some of them are probably not literally true, they can tell us what it means to be a Buddha and the sort of steps he must have gone through. So they have a mythic truth, and we can learn from them.

The life of the Buddha

The stories say that the boy who was to become the Buddha was born into a rich family – some say his father was a king, but more likely he was a man who had wealth and power in a state that was a republic. It is said that the Buddha-to-be was called Siddhartha and his family name was Gautama, and Gautama is what he is called in the earliest stories. His mother died soon after he was born, and his mother's sister married his father and brought him up.

Soon after Gautama's birth, a seer foretold that the boy would become either a great ruler or a great spiritual leader. His father wanted the boy to become a ruler, so provided a life of luxury and kept him away from anything that might distress him and tempt him to follow a spiritual life.

A story often told is that one day the Buddha-to-be rebelled against being kept in the palace, and went out in a chariot. He saw an old man, and realized that he and everyone he loved would become old. Another day, when he went out in his chariot, he saw someone who was sick and realized that he and those he loved could become ill. On a third day, when he went out in the chariot, he saw a corpse and realized that he and everyone he loved would die. These sights shook him and made the pleasures of the palace he lived in seem hollow. For a fourth time he went out in his chariot, and this time he saw a wanderer who was following a spiritual quest. The Buddha-to-be realized that this was what he needed to do in order to find a meaning to life that was not subject to old age, sickness, and death.

In our lives too, we are protected from old age, sickness, and death. People who appear in the media often wear make-up to make them look younger, those seriously sick are hidden from view in hospital, and we rarely see a dead body. We too can try to cover over the painful parts of life, and sometimes it can come as a shock when we see ourselves, or someone we know, ageing, becoming ill, or coming close to dying. For some people, such moments can initiate a change in priorities. I have a friend who thought she might die when she was involved in a road accident, and as a result she started coming along to a Buddhist centre and changed her job. My husband decided that he wanted to study medicine after his sister was diagnosed with a brain tumour and died.

Following his insights, the Buddha-to-be decided that he wanted to go forth from a life at home, that is to leave home and follow a spiritual quest. In those days, there were several possible ways to follow a spiritual quest. One was a path of meditation, and another was a path of austerities, which involved willingly taking on hardships such as depriving oneself of food or holding an uncomfortable posture for a long time. There are many different versions of what happened when the Buddha-to-be left home. In some he was young and unmarried and he may have left with his father's blessing, or his father and stepmother may have been in tears. Some say that he silently crept out. In other versions he was older and was married with a son.

When I first heard the story of the Buddha-to-be leaving his wife and child, I found it rather disturbing that he could do such a thing, but, in those versions of the story, his wife and child were looked after by the extended family. The Buddha did not forget his family and, shortly after he became enlightened, he returned and taught them what he had learned. Eventually his son, Rahula, became a monk, and his stepmother and wife became nuns and became enlightened themselves. But we are jumping ahead in the story, so let's return to the Buddha-to-be going forth from life at home.

In one text, the Buddha described his experience before he left home, and it sounds as if he was disillusioned with the life that his father led. He saw what was involved in living among others, and how living collectively can involve conflict around resources or status. We too can see how many people experience anxiety in their lives, especially when trying to achieve success at work.

> Fear is born from arming oneself.
> Just see how many people fight!
> I'll tell you about the dreadful fear
> that caused me to shake all over:
>
> Seeing creatures flopping around,
> Like fish in water too shallow,
> So hostile to one another!
> – Seeing this, I became afraid.[6]

Reflection

Bring to mind any moments when you have made major changes in your life or have considered such changes. Have there been particular events that have precipitated the desire to make a change in your life? Have concerns about the world led you to make any changes?

The fourth sight was a figure who provided a direction to go in. Is there someone you know or have heard of that you admire and would like to emulate? What are the qualities you see in them that you would like to develop in yourself?

The Buddha-to-be becomes a spiritual seeker

At the time Gautama, the Buddha-to-be, was living, there was a tradition of supporting people who were living a spiritual life. These spiritual seekers wandered around the countryside and were given food and other gifts by householders. They practised in various ways. Some meditated and some tried self-mortification, such as fasting or standing on one leg for a long period.

Gautama found a meditation teacher. His practice of meditation helped him to develop clear and calm mental states and bodily bliss. He practised so effectively that he was offered a share in the leadership of the group. Although he had experienced states of bliss, Gautama felt that he hadn't yet found what he was searching for and moved on. He found another teacher who helped him to go deeper in meditation, and experience even greater ecstasy and equanimity. Again, he was offered leadership of the group, but felt that there was further to go and moved on.

Then Gautama tried self-mortification with a group of five companions who were also practising austerities. He was very enthusiastic, and experimented with forceful mind control, controlling his breathing, and fasting. As a result, Gautama became extremely emaciated: 'Because of eating so little my ribs jutted out as gaunt as the crazy rafters of an old roofless barn.'[7] However, despite these strenuous efforts, he found that he had not reached the state of peace that he was searching for.

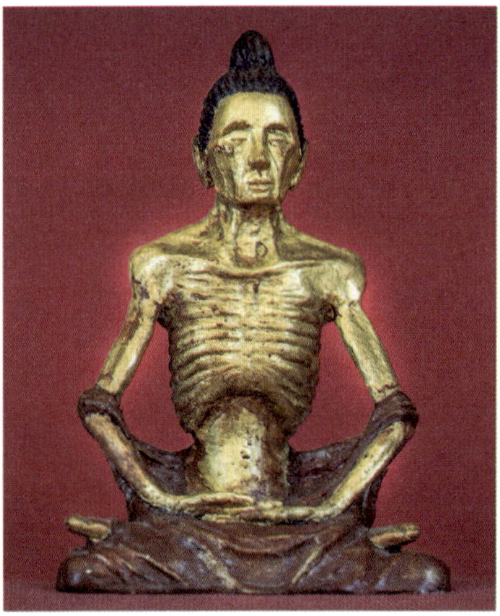

Once again, Gautama went forth, this time leaving behind such ascetic practices. He remembered a time when he was young and had sat under a rose apple tree watching his father ploughing. While he was sitting there, he had entered a very pleasant state of mind that was free from unwholesome experiences such as craving and aversion. He realized that meditative pleasure and happiness could be the way to Enlightenment.

So he decided to eat and, according to some stories, he took some rich rice pudding offered by a local girl. His five companions were disgusted that he had given up the practice of asceticism and left him. Gautama found an agreeable place under a bodhi tree near a river, and settled down determined to stay sitting until Enlightenment was reached.

Reflection

The Buddha realized that there are different kinds of pleasant experiences – some of which are wholesome and helpful, and some of which are unwholesome and unhelpful. For example, a pleasant experience arising from helping someone is wholesome, and a pleasant experience arising from outdoing someone else is unwholesome. Identify a pleasant experience that you have had that is wholesome. How might you experience this again or more?

Enlightenment and teaching

There are some wonderful stories told about what happened on the night of the Buddha's Enlightenment. They tell how Mara appeared. Mara can be regarded as the personification of all our negative tendencies, especially doubt. Mara tried to distract Gautama. One strategy he tried was to sow doubt in Gautama's mind that his practice was good enough for him to have the right to sit in that place and aim for Enlightenment. The story goes that Gautama touched the earth, and the earth goddess appeared and bore witness to all the practice that the Buddha-to-be had done. Some statues of the Buddha show this moment of touching the earth.

So Gautama continued to meditate under the bodhi tree, and gained Enlightenment and became the Buddha, the Awakened One. It is hard for us to imagine the magnitude of Enlightenment. In order to have a glimpse, let's explore some of the first words the Buddha is reported to have said afterwards. He used the simile of building a house for the way in which he had built an identity for himself. The house-builder is the part of him that constructed a self with which he could identify.

House-builder, now you are seen!
Never again shall you build me a house.
Your rafters are all broken,
your ridgepole shattered.
The mind, seeing things as they are,
has experienced the end of craving.[8]

The rafters can be taken as a simile for the passions, such as craving and aversion. The ridgepole stands for ignorance, the misconception, wrong views, and belief in the reality of an independent self that we hold, but which are misleading. Let's explore what this might mean. The most significant assumptions are about ourselves and other people. For example, I can think of myself as being a woman, a wife and mother, a Buddhist, of being old, and so on. These labels are true to some extent, but they can carry assumptions about what I can and can't do. For example, when I was young I studied maths, and this was considered by some people, and even by me to some extent, to be an odd choice for a girl. When I think of myself as being old, it is easy to assume that I can't learn something new. Every identification brings a certain restriction to what it feels all right to do.

Even if they are not restrictive, identifications can cause pain because we are tempted to defend them, or they are unrealistic and give us a falsely positive – or negative – view of ourselves and we are disappointed when life shows us that we are wrong. We are all changing, and our ideas may make us resist change in ourselves and others.

Letting go of these identifications, or at least holding them lightly, gives more freedom. For me, it can be a delight to behave like a child with simple pleasures and play, so not being constrained by assumptions that I or others may have. The Buddha at his Enlightenment was letting go of – or holding lightly to – all possible identifications. For that reason, he was called 'the trackless one', as it was impossible to make assumptions about what he would or would not do.

Reflection

I invite you to explore the ways in which you tend to describe yourself. You can do this by finding different endings to the following sentences:

- I am a ...
- I am the sort of person who ...
- I am not ...
- I am not the sort of person who ...

You may like to ask yourself to what extent each of your descriptions is true.

Some identifications may be helpful to us when we are starting on the Buddhist path. For example, I have found it helpful to think of myself as a meditator, as it has made it easier to establish a meditation habit. However, I have found it helpful to hold this identity lightly when I'm ill and may not be able to sit in meditation. In those circumstances, it may only be possible to relax into lying on the bed, and it is helpful if I don't give myself a hard time about the limitations.

Some identifications can be unhelpful though, as they restrict what we think we can do. For example, you may identify with your job and so not consider doing something that is more satisfying. Are there any of your identifications you think it would be helpful to drop or hold more lightly?

After his Enlightenment, the Buddha spent some time first sitting and absorbing what had happened, and then reflecting and deciding to communicate to others what he had learned. He first thought of the two men who had taught him to meditate, but he realized that they were both dead. So he went to find the five ascetics who had been his companions. Once he found them, he

spent some time teaching them and he helped them to become enlightened too.

The Buddha spent the following forty-five years wandering around northern India and teaching. During that time, he gained many disciples. One of his disciples, Ananda, became his attendant for the last twenty-five years of his life. Reading and writing weren't widespread at the time, and it's possible that the Buddha didn't know how to write. So none of the teachings were written down, and instead they were recited over and over again, so that they were remembered and passed on. Ananda was excellent at remembering, and tradition has it that many of the teachings that have been passed down have come via him.

The Buddha died from food poisoning when he was aged about eighty. He had said that it was impossible to say what happens to enlightened beings once their bodies have died. He clearly would not exist after death in the same way as he was before he died. However, his ideas and teachings continued to circulate, and his wisdom and compassion continued in his disciples, so there was something about him that carried on.

When the Buddha died, his enlightened disciples didn't weep, but the unenlightened disciples did. Perhaps the enlightened disciples had deeply absorbed the insight that everything is impermanent. Perhaps they had a sense that something of the Buddha continued to live within them, and also that whatever emotions they felt were changing. With their Enlightenment had come a profound equanimity.

What was the Buddha like?

You will have seen many images of the Buddha, including those from earlier in this chapter. There are no images from around the time of the Buddha: for a long time after his death, he was usually just represented by a footprint, a bodhi tree, or an empty chair. The images we see today are trying to show his qualities. Most of them depict someone who is at peace and gently smiling. Many of the images show him with a bump on the top of his head. This bump has come to indicate that the image shows the Buddha rather in the way that a crown is used to indicate a king. Kings nowadays rarely wear a crown, just as the Buddha didn't actually have a protuberance on his head, at least as far as we know. Many images show the Buddha meditating.

Images of the Buddha don't just show him sitting. You have already seen one of him lying down, and there are images showing him standing as well. Images vary a lot according to the time and place in which they were made. People usually depict the Buddha to look a bit like themselves! There are various images in this chapter, and you may like to search elsewhere for ones that you find inspiring. I loved the enormous Amitabha Buddha that stands at the north stairs in the British Museum even before I became very interested in Buddhism.

Reflection

Which image of the Buddha particularly appeals to you?

We know nothing for certain about the historical Buddha, but we can have a flavour of what he was like from the earliest scriptures. From what we know, the Buddha usually spent the morning on an alms round in the nearest town or village, collecting food in his bowl. He ate just one meal a day at noon. At one time, a brahmin student observed his daily conduct. This is what he reported.

> After the meal, at noon, he puts away his robe and bowl, washes his hands and feet, and with a sitting mat over his shoulder enters a hut to sit in meditation.[9]

We also hear that the Buddha often taught whoever was with him; sometimes he enjoyed going off into the forest alone, and sometimes he would accept invitations to eat with his lay followers.

It is clear that the presence of the Buddha had a big effect on people. This is the experience of one man, Bahiya, who was searching for the Buddha and found him on his alms round (in the early texts, the Buddha is often called 'The Blessed One'):

> Then Bahiya saw the Blessed One going for alms in Savatthi – pleasing, lovely to see, with calmed senses and tranquil mind, attained to perfect poise and calm, controlled, a perfected one, watchful with restrained senses.[10]

The Buddha cared about the welfare of the people who followed him. When he visited three of them who were practising together, his first words were

> I hope you are all keeping well, Anuruddha, I hope you are all comfortable, I hope you are not having any trouble getting almsfood.

He clearly valued harmony, because, after hearing that all was well, he then went on to say:

> I hope, Anuruddha, that you are all living in concord, with mutual appreciation, without disputing, blending like milk and water, viewing each other with kindly eyes.[11]

There are times when his disciples were quarrelling, and the Buddha would admonish them; if the quarrelling continued, he would go off by himself into the forest.

The Buddha took delight in praising his followers. One night, some of his senior disciples were in a beautiful wood in the moonlight with the trees in blossom, and with scents floating in the air. They asked each other what sort of follower would illuminate the wood. Each disciple gave a different reply to the others. As an example, Ananda replied that it was one who

> has learned much, remembers what he has learned, and consolidates what he has learned. Such teachings as are good in the beginning, good in the middle, and good in the end, with the right meaning and phrasing, and which affirm a holy life that is utterly perfect and pure - such teachings as these he has learned much of, remembered, mastered verbally, investigated with the mind, and penetrated well by view. And he teaches the Dhamma to the four assemblies with well-rounded and coherent statements and phrases for the eradication of the underlying tendencies.[12]

When the Buddha heard what Ananda had said he replied,

> Ananda, speaking rightly, should speak just as he did. For Ananda has learned much, remembers what he has learned, and consolidates what he has learned. Such teachings as are good in the beginning, good in the middle, and good in the end, with the right meaning and phrasing, and which affirm a holy life that is utterly perfect and pure - such teachings as these he has learned much of, remembered, mastered verbally, investigated with the mind, and penetrated well by view. And he teaches the Dhamma to the four assemblies with well-rounded and coherent statements and phrases for the eradication of the underlying tendencies.[13]

The Buddha similarly praised each of the disciples for their particular way of practising. They were all different, with one delighting in solitary meditation, one having a divine eye that enabled him to see a thousand worlds, one living in the forest with few wants, one enjoying discussing the Dharma with others, and one having mastery over his mind. The Buddha said of each of them that they practised as they should.

Reflection

In what way do you or would you particularly like to practise? Is it study, or meditation, or sharing experience with others, or ...?

What aspects of the Dharma are you particularly drawn to? Is it a search for truth, or a way of working with your mind, or meditation, or a community of people who share your values, or solitude, or ...?

What qualities do you see yourself developing? Perhaps clarity, or kindness, or adventure, or finding freedom and meaning, or ...?

There are many other times when the Buddha praised the practice of an individual or of the group of followers he was with. For example, here is a time when he praised the company of his followers, called 'bhikkhus,' who were practising together:

> Bhikkhus, this assembly is free from prattle, this assembly is free from chatter. It consists purely of heartwood. Such is this Sangha of bhikkhus, such is this assembly. Such an assembly as is worthy of gifts, worthy of hospitality, worthy of offerings, worthy of reverential salutation, an incomparable field of merit for the world – such is this Sangha of bhikkhus, such is this assembly. Such an assembly that a small gift given to it becomes great and a great gift greater – such is this Sangha of bhikkhus, such is this assembly. Such an assembly as is rare for the world to see – such is this Sangha of bhikkhus, such is this assembly. Such an assembly as would be worth journeying many leagues with a travel-bag to see – such is this Sangha of bhikkhus, such is this assembly.[14]

At one time, someone asked the Buddha what a perfect person would be like, and the reply probably gives a sense of the Buddha's qualities:

> A person who is calmed, who has extinguished all their cravings before the time their body disintegrates into nothing, who has no concern with how things began or with how they will end and no fixation with what happens in between: such a one has no preferences.
>
> They have no anger, no fear and no pride. Nothing disturbs their composure and nothing gives them cause for regret. They are the wise ones who are restrained in speech.
>
> They have no longing for the future and no grief for the past; there are no views or opinions that lead them. They are detached from the entangled world of sense-impression.
>
> They do not conceal anything and there is nothing they hold on to. Without acquisitiveness or envy, they remain unobtrusive; they have no disdain or insult for anyone.
>
> They are not someone who is full of themselves, or who is addicted to pleasure; they are gentle and alert, with no blind faith; they show no aversion to anything.
>
> They do not work because they want something; if they get nothing at all they remain unperturbed. There is no craving to build up the passion to taste new pleasures.
>
> Their mindfulness holds them poised in a constant even-mindedness where arrogance is impossible; they make no comparisons with the rest of the world as 'superior', 'inferior' or 'equal'.
>
> Because they understand the Way Things Are, they are free from dependency and there is nothing they rely on. For them there is no more craving to exist or not to exist.
>
> This is what I call a person who is calmed.[15]

Reflection

What interests you in this description? What do you respond to? Do you know people with some of these qualities? Can you see yourself in some of these statements, at least to some degree?

There is a danger, in reading this list of qualities, that we can feel completely inadequate, or we might get the impression that we ought not to feel anger and fear, which can be disconcerting since they arise when we don't want them to. It can be unhelpful to try to force them to go away. Many of us have a tendency to be excessively critical of ourselves, and, if that is true for you, it may be helpful to realize that you are not alone, and that criticisms are one of the challenges of being human. We shall be exploring some practices that can help in later chapters.

It's also interesting to notice how others responded to the Buddha. Here is an example of a king who had clearly heard about what the Buddha was doing:

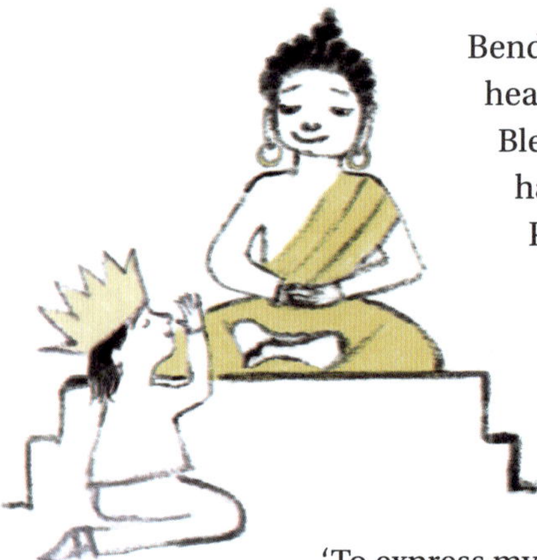

> Bending low before the Blessed One, with his head on the ground, King Pasenadi kissed the Blessed One's feet embracing them with his hands. Then he announced his name: 'I am Pasenadi, Lord, the Kosala King.'
>
> 'But, great king, what reason do you see for showing to this body such profound humility and offering it such loving devotion?'
>
> 'To express my grateful thanks, Lord: for that reason do I show to the Blessed One such profound humility and offer to him my loving devotion.

> 'For the Blessed One, Lord, lives for the welfare of the multitude, for the happiness of the multitude; because a great many people have been established by him in the holy method of the Teaching, namely, in noble and beautiful principles. It is for this reason, Lord, that I show to the Blessed One such profound humility and offer him my loving devotion.'[16]

Pingiya was an old man who travelled a long way to see the Buddha. When he returned home, he talked about his experience and described the Buddha in this way:

> a mammoth of knowledge and completely pure, a man without desire.
>
> When a voice has none of the glibness of pride and none of the ingrained stains of ignorance, then its words are full of sweetness and beauty. It is such words that I praise now...
>
> a teacher whose Dharma is the Way Things Are, instant, immediate and visible all around, eroding desire without harmful side-effects, with nothing else quite like it anywhere in the world.[17]

Reflection

What qualities that you have heard about in this chapter do you particularly admire? Have you encountered a picture or statue of the Buddha that captures some of these qualities?

Pingiya also described very poetically the effect that the teachings had on him:

> It is like a bird that leaves the bushes of the scrubland and flies to the fruit trees of the forest. I too have left the bleary half-light of opinions; like a swan I have reached a great lake.[18]

There is a set of phrases that many people used after hearing the Buddha:

> Master Gautama has made the Dhamma clear in many ways, as though he were turning upright what had been overthrown, revealing what was hidden, showing the way to one who was lost, or holding up a lamp in the darkness so those with good eyesight can see forms.[19]

They go on to talk about 'going for refuge':

> I now go for refuge to Master Gautama, to the Dhamma, and to the Sangha of bhikkhus.[20]

So the Buddha clearly had a very profound effect on many of the people who heard him teach. They saw things differently and felt changed, and wanted to commit themselves to the three jewels by following the Buddha, putting his teachings into practice, and becoming part of the community of the Buddha's followers.

Reflection

What is it like to admire someone, be drawn to them and know that they have capacities and qualities we would like to develop?

In those days, people talked about committing themselves in terms of 'going for refuge'. The term 'going for refuge' can seem rather foreign to us, and I certainly found it difficult to relate to it when I first met it. It refers to what is important to us, what we place our heart upon, and what gives us a sense of security. In the Triratna Buddhist Community, we talk about going for refuge to the three jewels as being the essential act of a Buddhist. When I first thought about that, I realized that what was important to me was primarily my husband, my family, and my job. Of course, none of these can be relied upon because I could lose them all. I no longer have a job, but husband and family are still an important part of my life. However, the teachings of the Buddha are now very much more significant; my practice is based on a direction provided by the Buddha, and I obtain a lot of support from companions in the spiritual life. These give a much firmer sense of security, as, whatever happens, I know how to practise.

Reflection

What is important to you in your life and gives a sense of security?

One question that intrigues me is how a Buddha would live in our modern society. It would be hard to pursue the same lifestyle as the Buddha did all those thousands of years ago. Could they live with the solitude they wanted and yet close enough to a town or city to be provided with food? If they lived in a colder climate, they would need shelter in winter. Could they have the conditions they needed for practice without handling money?

We have to use our imagination to have a sense of possibilities for the way a Buddha could live. A contemporary Buddhist, Srivati, wrote the poem below. I love the way she imagines what it would be like to take the Buddha to a supermarket.

Shopping with the Buddha
(After Billy Collins)

He seemed to enjoy the drive.
Not so much the view,
although I noticed him noticing the man
stood in the allotment
as we turned left towards Asda.
No, it was the breeze.
He leant his head out of the window

like a dog, closing his eyes sometimes
to inhale the world.

As I pulled into the parking space
and turned off the engine
he was already opening the door
and making for the trolleys.
A few people turned to stare,
but not many.
This is East London after all.
My surprise was that he didn't know
that he needed a pound coin.
I assumed omniscience;
He assumed freedom and trust.

I let him push the trolley.
How could I have stopped him?
He had already refolded his robe across his shoulder
and was off into the vast cavern.
Knowing we needed vegetables,
another assumption:
that we would focus on our needs,
move mindfully, no energy (or money) wasted,
and be done in half an hour.

But no. The Buddha wanted to see everything.
We walked up and down every aisle
so that he could marvel
at the choice of breakfast cereals,
taste the free samples of cheese at the deli counter
and stand quietly by the banks of chilled flesh,
his bare shoulder goose-bumping
before he moved on.

For a while I lost him.
Then hearing a distant, deep laughter,
saw a flash of flying saffron
as he go-karted the trolley down the middle aisle
towards the shelves of eggs.
He stopped like a professional,
delighted to discover the button for bored children:

one press and a chicken crows like morning.
He pressed it three times.

I love the Buddha,
even when we reached the checkout
and discovered the expensive chocolate cake
he'd put in the trolley,
and knew that he had no money.

As we put the shopping bags into the boot of the car
I realised that we hadn't spoken once.
'Did you enjoy that?' I said.
'I enjoy everything,' he replied.[21]

Reflection

We have been exploring the qualities of the Buddha because he is an ideal and gives us a sense of direction. However, contemplating an ideal can bring challenges, as the following reflection shows.

Step 1: We have seen many descriptions of the Buddha. Choose one quality of the Buddha that you would like to have. Contemplate what that quality you want is like. What is it like to be with that quality and to contemplate it? Then notice how you feel.

Step 2: Bring to mind a positive quality that you have already, at least to some extent. You don't have to be perfect, but you already have it to a greater extent than you did when you were a child. Reflect on how you have changed in that respect. Now notice how you feel.

Step 3: Now keep in mind the quality you chose in step 2, which you have already, and then bring to mind the quality from step 1 that you decided you want to have. So you have both qualities in mind. How do you feel when you do that?

Commentary

Step 1: a quality you would like to have

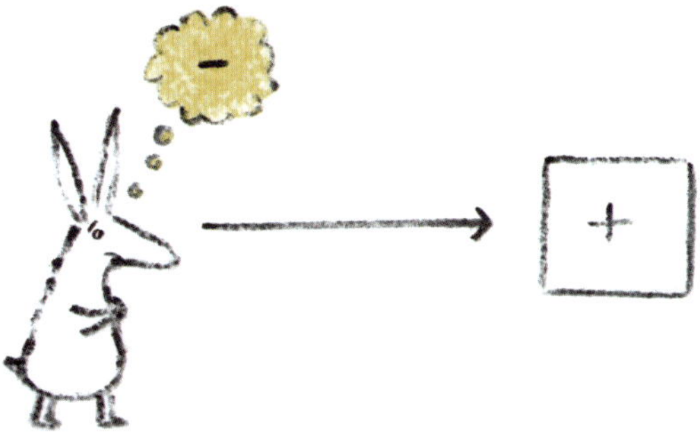

Although you are thinking of the quality that you wish to have, in order to identify a quality to develop you attend to some lack in your experience. That lack may feel *discouraging*. Also, the desired quality is only a future possibility while the lack is experienced as a reality in the present.

Step 2: a positive quality you have already developed (at least to some extent)

You may feel *more confident* when experiencing a quality that you have already. However, there is the danger of passivity and complacency, so it's better to proceed with step 3.

Step 3: first bringing to mind a quality you have already (as in step 2) … and *then* bringing to mind the quality (from step 1) that you would like to develop

If you keep in mind what you already have, then you may feel *more confident about developing* something new.

This exercise illustrates the danger there can be in focusing on a goal, or the person we want to be. It is very easy to become discouraged by our failures to live up to that goal. In his book *Happier*,[22] the psychology professor Tal Ben-Shahar says that attaining lasting happiness requires that we enjoy the journey on our way towards a destination we deem valuable. Happiness is not about making it to the peak of the mountain, nor is it about climbing aimlessly around the mountain: happiness is the experience of climbing towards the peak.

Something similar can be said about our journey on the Buddhist path. So, for most of us, it can be very helpful both to have a sense of the direction in which we want to go and to focus on what we are doing that is supportive. This helps us to enjoy the path, and gives us the confidence to make further positive changes.

3 The Teachings of the Buddha

We are now going to explore what the Buddha realized at his Enlightenment, at least as far as we are able, and how he went about communicating it. This is an ambitious aim. We shall start by exploring an example from our own experience.

You are probably familiar with feeling stress sometimes. What factors lead you to feeling stressed? For me, the most common factors are feeling criticized, feeling time pressure, having lots of things that need to be done, lack of sleep, lack of exercise, and feeling a lack of control. It's possible to draw a diagram to illustrate this.[23]

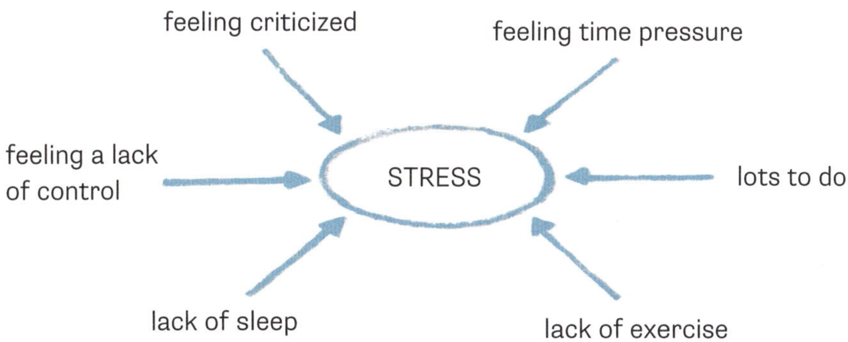

You may well find that similar factors affect you. Most if not all of these arrows also go the other way. So, when stressed, it is more likely that I will sleep badly. Also, it is more likely that I'll feel time pressure and be more sensitive to what people say, and so feel criticized.

The factors also often affect each other, so, when there is a lot to do, I'm more likely to feel time pressure and not take exercise. When I fail to take some exercise, it's more likely that I'll sleep badly. Many of these arrows go both ways too, so feeling time pressure will also make me feel that there is a lot to do. In the following diagram, there are lots more arrows that I'm aware of in my experience. You may see some additional ones that are true for you.

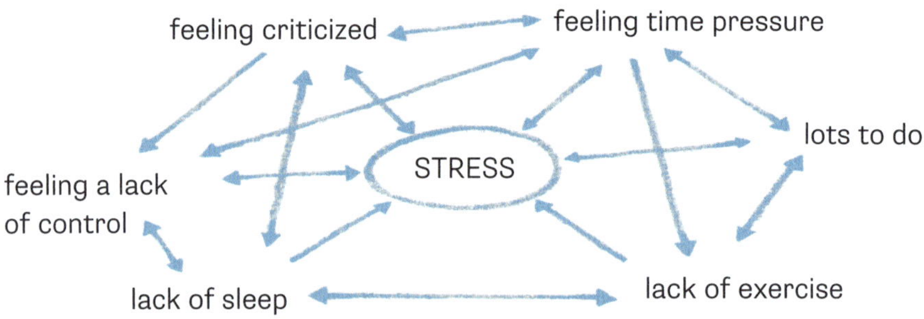

So there are many factors that contribute to stress. They interact, and stress tends to make them worse, so they mutually reinforce each other. It may not feel like it, but this is good news, because, if we can change any one of the factors, then we change all of them. So if I take regular exercise, then it makes a difference to all the other factors. This can feel counterintuitive. I found something like this when I started meditating regularly. In order to fit meditation into my morning schedule, I needed to wake up earlier, and yet I found that I had more energy in the evening. This was totally unexpected and very welcome.

Activity

Draw a diagram like the one above, showing the main factors that cause you to feel stressed and arrows showing how they interact.

Is there one of the factors that you could change?

It is natural to focus on what is wrong, but it can be helpful as well to look at the positive. This is done in the next activity.

Activity

Draw a similar diagram showing the factors that nourish you. Draw arrows between the factors to show how they influence each other.

At the heart of the teachings of the Buddha is the idea that everything arises because of conditions. This is called 'dependent arising' or 'conditioned co-arising'. The second translation is not as accurate, but it does make it more obvious that conditions can often mutually reinforce each other. The Buddha gave a simple formula for conditionality, as follows:

> This being, that becomes;
> from the arising of this, that arises.
> This not being, that does not become;
> from the ceasing of this, that ceases.[24]

It could be said more simply as, 'Things arise because of conditions and cease when those conditions cease.' By exploring how our experience is affected by conditions, we can find out how stress arises for us, and that can help us to know how the experience of stress can be transformed. Dependent arising is a way of expressing the intellectual content of the Enlightenment experience, as far as we can understand it. The Buddha described this teaching as being 'deep, delicate, and subtle', and he equated it with the Dharma, that is with the essence of his teaching.

It may be that dependent arising seems obvious to you, especially if you have a scientific background. Ananda certainly felt like that at one time:

> The Venerable Ananda approached the Buddha and, on arrival, having bowed down to the Buddha, sat to one side. As he was sitting there he said to the Buddha: 'It's amazing, lord, it's astounding, how deep this conditioned co-production is, and how deep its appearance, and yet to me it seems as clear as clear can be.'
>
> [The Buddha:] 'Don't say that, Ananda. Don't say that. Deep is this conditioned co-production, and deep its appearance. It's because of not understanding and not penetrating this teaching that this generation is like a tangled skein, a knotted ball of string, like matted rushes and reeds, and does not go beyond suffering.'[25]

In the past, if I argued with a friend, my mind would feel like a knotted ball of string. Thoughts went round and round and I realized that I was thinking similar thoughts over and over again, and found it difficult to stop. Sometimes the thoughts were blaming my friend and sometimes they were blaming myself, and often there were more and more stories that I was telling and I felt more and more unhappy. Escape only came when I stepped back and could see things with a different state of mind and with a bigger perspective, seeing more of the many factors that influenced our communication. So I would remember that one of us or both of us were tired or that one of us was in pain. Then the difficulty seemed less personal, and I could feel less defensive and better able to see their point of view.

Reflection

Recall a time when you had a difficulty with someone. Did your mind have a tendency to go round and round when the difficulty was live? Is it different now?

Now let's explore conditionality further by looking at an experience I had many years ago. I was on retreat by myself near the sea, and was studying a book about conditionality and systems theory. Every day I walked to the sea and simply spent some time enjoying being there. This is a photograph showing how it was.

I read about how something new can arise from factors interacting and giving positive feedback, and longed for a simple example so that I could understand it better. That day, when I went to the beach, instead of the beach sloping uniformly down to the sea, there were small bays that made a scalloped edge.

When I looked closely, I could see that each wave lifted up small pebbles as it came in, and if these landed on a relatively high place, then they stayed there as the sea went out again. If they landed on a low place, then the sea pulled them back as it went out again. So the pattern became stronger and stronger. The sea shaped the beach, and also the beach shaped the way in which the waves of the sea broke. The sea and beach could not be separated: not only did they affect each other, there were always pebbles and sand being carried by the sea. It didn't stop there. The beach was shaped by the crumbling cliffs and the cliffs by the sea and the wind and rain, and the wind and rain affected the sea too.

So it became clear that everything was changing and nothing was separate from everything else. The Buddhist tradition often expresses this lack of separation by saying that something is 'empty', which is short for being empty of individual selfhood – for example, there is no beach without the sea.

Of course, we are much more interested in our minds and experience than in the sea, but these properties apply there too. For us, change means that we can grow and develop, and being empty means that we are shaped by the conditions we are in. Another aspect worth keeping in mind is that everything we do makes a difference, not just to us, but also to others – much more so than we imagine. To help with understanding the far-reaching consequences of these insights, let's look at a few examples.

- In our society, achievements are usually credited to a single individual, although the individual built on the achievements of others. Isaac Newton realized this and said, 'If I have seen further, it is by standing on the shoulders of giants.'
- In a similar way, I'm aware that I could only write this book because of the many people who taught me, who wrote books I have read, who talked to me and shared their insights, and more mundanely who grew the food I have eaten, made the clothes I wear, and produced the power that has kept me warm, not to mention those who have given me love, support, and encouragement over the years.

- It's easy to think that, if we meditate in the morning or do some exercise, then that only affects us, but it makes a difference to our mental state and that affects everyone we meet, and then affects the people they meet.
- When I have made a mistake, I can feel a lot of shame. It can help to realize that I'm not the same person now, as I have learned from my mistake.

Activity

Find and explore other examples where you or other people have not taken a full account of change and interconnectedness.

Reflection

Let's do a reflection on change that can help us in taking a bigger perspective on our lives.

- Start by bringing kind awareness to parts of the body in turn, such as the feet, the legs, the torso, the hands, the arms, and the head.
- Now focusing on a part of the body that feels particularly good and letting that feeling spread to other parts of the body - you may like to imagine light or warmth spreading through the body.
- Then remembering a time in the past when you were learning something you make use of now, perhaps how to drive a car, ride a bike, or use a computer. Bring an attitude of gratitude to yourself then for making the effort.
- Then thinking back to a time when you were struggling, and telling the you then how it will pass.

- Now imagining yourself further developed in the future in a way you want to be, and let that person wish your present self well and thank you for the effort you are making now.
- To finish, sitting in the present with an appreciation of the whole body.

The four noble truths

One of the most important consequences of conditionality is the teaching of the four noble truths. These truths are 'noble' because anyone who fully understands them can be regarded as noble. They were taught by the Buddha many times. Although they are commonly known as 'truths,' you could also call them 'realities.' They are:

1. the truth of suffering;
2. the truth of the origin of suffering;
3. the truth of the cessation of suffering;
4. the truth of a path leading to the cessation of suffering.

These can be paraphrased briefly as:

1. We encounter unhappiness of various kinds during our lives.
2. Our distress is mainly caused by denying that things are the way they are or by turning away from things as they are.
3. It's possible to be free of this distress.
4. The path to being free involves acting with kindness, meditating, and taking a wise view.

The first truth

Now let's look at these truths more deeply. The first one says that our lives contain *dukkha*. 'Dukkha' is a hard word to translate into English. It's often translated as 'suffering,' but, although suffering is dukkha, it is too strong to encompass everything covered by the word 'dukkha'. Some people translate 'dukkha' as 'unsatisfactory', but that is too weak to encompass it all. Dukkha encompasses the complete spectrum of unsatisfactoriness, stress, suffering, pain, and distress, so I'm going to leave it untranslated. The Buddha said of it:

> This is the noble truth of dukkha: birth is dukkha, ageing is dukkha, death is dukkha; sorrow, lamentation, pain, grief, and despair are dukkha; association with the unbeloved is dukkha; separation from the loved is dukkha; not getting what is wanted is dukkha.[26]

This truth is not saying that all of life is suffering; some people think this is what the Buddha taught, though he didn't. It is saying that life is unsatisfactory in many ways and doesn't always go the way we want it to. Dukkha is built into the way in which we experience life. In order to stay alive, our ancestors needed to keep themselves free from dangers and find resources such as food and water. In order to be skilled at staying free from danger and finding resources, they needed to remember significant events in their past and plan for the future. Staying free from danger was particularly important, as they would not survive missing a lion in the bushes; it was less important to notice an apple on a tree. So we too watch out for potential dangers all the time. It is little wonder that so many of us suffer from anxiety. Even when life is going well, we can be concerned that the good times are going to end. So dukkha forms part of our lives even if it is not always present.

For each of the truths, the Buddha gave us a task. For this first truth, he said that dukkha is to be understood. As a first step, this means being aware that we are experiencing dukkha when that is what is happening. It may be that there is some discomfort in the body or some irritation or frustration in the mind. Just knowing that the discomfort or irritation is present can be helpful.

Much of the time, most of us distract ourselves and don't allow ourselves to be aware of dukkha. For example, I once took on a practice of being more aware of body sensations when getting dressed, and was surprised to find that the clothes felt cold and this was unpleasant. You may think that it is a good idea not to experience what is unpleasant, but, when we have a habit of ignoring unpleasant experiences, we also start to ignore the pleasant experiences. I was also not noticing times when my body felt pleasantly warm. This lack of awareness can lead us into a state where we are only half living. George Eliot puts it rather better than I can:

> If we had a keen vision and feeling of all ordinary human life, it would be like hearing the grass grow and the squirrel's heart beat, and we should die of that roar which lies on the other side of silence.[27]

Activity

Spend a minute becoming aware of any dukkha that you are experiencing at the moment, either in the body or in the mind. Notice if your mind or thoughts keep trying to run away with you, or if your body tenses when you notice the dukkha. As best you can, relax and bring some kindness to what you are experiencing.

The second truth

The second truth says that there is an origin for our dukkha, namely craving. It is perfectly natural to want certain necessities, such as food, a comfortable temperature, and to feel safe. Dukkha can come when we crave for something that can't give us what we want it to give, for example when we try to distract ourselves from feelings of stress or loneliness by eating chocolate or shopping or watching television. Even if these behaviours provide temporary relief, I find that the underlying dissatisfaction tends to reassert itself, and added to it is an unpleasant feeling from having eaten so much I feel a bit sick, or having spent more money than was wise, or not really enjoying the programmes I have been watching. None of these activities is inherently wrong. The problem is using them to try to smother unpleasant experience.

Desire is not the problem, but believing that your happiness depends on getting what you want is. We all of us have times when things don't work out the way we want. It may rain when we want to go out for a walk, or someone may criticize us. It is natural to feel disappointment or anger in these circumstances. However, holding on to these feelings, and even encouraging them, does bring dukkha. As Oprah Winfrey says, 'What I've learned about being angry with people is that it generally hurts you more than it hurts them.' We can't just wish the feelings away though. There are two possible approaches. One approach is to let the feelings cool, just as we might patiently wait for a cup of tea to cool down. The other is to notice the effect of our thoughts and how they may be driving our emotions. We have some choice about the emotions we experience, because we can change the conditions involved. So we might find something fun to do indoors when it is raining.

There are circumstances where it is unhelpful to get caught up in negative emotions, but it is important to keep acting in a way that helps to bring about positive change. So we may need to do what we can to prevent violence towards ourselves or others. I can feel frustration that what I do makes little difference to climate problems, but nevertheless I find a satisfaction from knowing that I'm doing what I can. At least I can feel good about my own behaviour, and that brings a certain peace of mind.

There are some desires that are positive, such as wanting to have deep meditations. However, even in that case, being distressed when that doesn't happen is unhelpful. It is an example of something around which we need to set up supportive conditions and then relax about the outcome. So we need acceptance married with knowledge and understanding. Here again, there are no simple answers about what to do.

The Buddha talked about how the task we have with this truth is to let go of unhelpful craving. I prefer the language of 'letting be', as it doesn't mean pushing away emotions that have arisen. Also, this truth isn't saying that we don't try for a particular outcome that we want. It does mean that when the outcome is not what we desire, then we need to assess what is a wise course of action. The following short activity can be helpful. It is an adaptation of an activity that Ruth A. Baer gives in her book *Practising Happiness*, and it helps with letting be in a stressful situation. You can remember it by the acronym SOBER.[28]

Activity: SOBER

S	Stop		Pause in what you are doing and adjust your posture to be dignified and relaxed.
O	Observe		Notice the sensations in the body, thoughts, feelings/emotions, and urges/impulses that are happening, perhaps putting the experiences into words.
B	Breathe		Attend gently to your breathing, just focusing on the sensations of breathing for one or two minutes (perhaps counting ten breaths). If the mind wanders, then briefly acknowledging and labelling your experience, for example, as planning or daydreaming, before gently returning to the breath sensations as an anchor in the present moment.
E	Expand awareness		Become aware of the whole body, perhaps breathing into any uncomfortable sensations, and allowing your experience to be as it is. You may like to say to yourself, 'It's OK for me to feel this.'
R	Respond mindfully		There are several possibilities here. You could simply hold your experience in a broad awareness and allow it to be, and let a situation or feeling run its course. At other times you may need to take more definite action.

This breathing space allows you to remember what you care about and notice what the situation requires.

The third truth

The third truth says that there can be cessation or transcendence of suffering. So it is possible for craving and reactivity to cease. We shall still be able to experience what is unpleasant, but it won't disturb us. Our mind is willing to be with whatever is present without being disturbed by it. The Buddha describes it like this.

> Enraptured with lust, enraged with anger, blinded by delusion, overwhelmed, with mind obsessed, people aim at their own ruin, or at the ruin of others, or at the ruin of both, and they experience mental pain and grief. But if lust, anger, and delusion are given up, they aim neither at their own ruin, nor at the ruin of others, nor at the ruin of both, and they experience no mental pain and grief. Thus is Enlightenment visible in this life, immediate, inviting, attractive, and personally experienced by the wise.[29]

The task the Buddha gives of realizing this truth is not easy, as it involves becoming enlightened. However, the next truth gives us a way of moving in that direction. Also, we can have glimpses, and you may have done so already. I have always been encouraged by observing those who have been practising longer than me and seeing how they are more contented, kinder, and wiser than me. The direction these people are going in seems worth following.

Reflection

Recollect any times when you have felt particularly contented. What conditions helped that contentment to arise?

The fourth truth

The fourth truth says that the noble eightfold path is the way leading to the cessation of dukkha. After the next reflection, we shall explore this path in some detail, as it has the power to change our lives. The task is to cultivate this path.

Reflection

William Blake's poem 'Eternity' expresses the four truths or realities in a slightly different order. Can you see the connection?

> He who binds to himself a joy
> Does the winged life destroy
> He who kisses the joy as it flies
> Lives in eternity's sunrise.[30]

The noble eightfold path

We can think of the eightfold path as being like the converse of the stress diagram we met above. Each limb of the path, when practised, reduces the suffering we experience. Furthermore, the limbs interact with each other, so developing one of them also develops the others. The arrows aren't all shown as the diagram would become too complex.

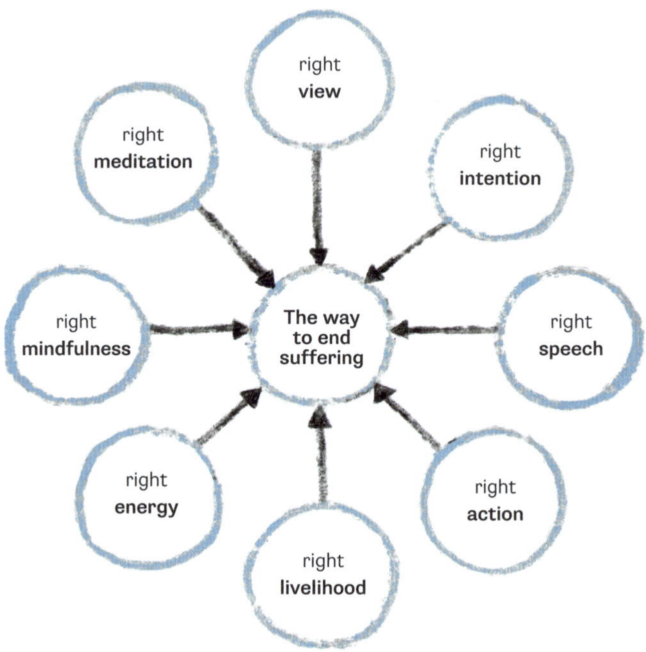

The path is symbolized by an eight-spoked wheel known as a dharmachakra. Each of the eight sections or 'limbs' is described as 'right'. The word 'right' translates the Pali word *samma*, which means something like 'whole', 'complete', 'integral', emphasizing that all the limbs are practised interdependently with each other. So, for example, mindfulness is only *right* mindfulness when it incorporates an intention to be kind and actions that are ethical. However mindful you are when robbing a bank, that is not *right* mindfulness.

Right view

Right view involves understanding experience from the viewpoint of the four noble truths. So it involves being aware of the ways in which we suffer and how we can change to relieve that suffering.

Another aspect is having insight into the three *lakshana*s or characteristics of conditioned existence.

1. All conditioned things are impermanent or changing. We have already explored this to some extent by exploring how the sea and beach were interacting. More interesting is seeing how our experience changes, even in simple ways, such as noticing how one piece of chocolate may be delicious, but the second much less so. Or you may notice how the meaning you take from an email can change from one day to the next as you read it in a different state of mind.

2. All conditioned things are dukkha or unsatisfactory. Dukkha arises from impermanence. Even if everything is going well for a while, this is bound to change. Everyone ages, becomes sick, and eventually dies, so we cannot depend on anyone or anything to bring us lasting safety and happiness. Even when things are going well and we are feeling happy, we can feel some subtle, or sometimes not so subtle, anxiety that they will change. Only Enlightenment can bring ultimate happiness that is deeper and doesn't go away.

3. Nothing has an independent unchanging existence. Everything is connected to everything else. This is becoming clearer and clearer in ecosystems as we come to understand

them better and better. As an example, let's explore what happened when wolves were reintroduced to Yellowstone National Park. It changed the behaviour of the elk, who spent more time on higher ground so that they could spot the wolves. This led to aspens, willows, and other vegetation flourishing on lower ground, which meant that beavers flourished, improving the wetlands. Flowers grew on the stream banks that fed insects, which provided food for songbirds. Also, the water was more shaded, so it was clearer and better for aquatic insects, so there were more trout. It is rather surprising that introducing wolves led to more trout.

We too are constantly shaped by our past and by the conditions we are currently in, for example, by the food we eat, by the quality of the air we breathe, by the beauty of our environment, by the states of mind of the people we come into contact with, by the work we do, and so on. In return, we influence each of these conditions. For example, our choices of food influence what the shops stock and farmers grow; our states of mind influence how people respond to us. It's like an extremely complex dance that never stops.

Reflection

What aspects of your life do you have complete control over? What aspects can you influence even if you are unable to control them?

If we can appreciate this dance more fully, we'll not think so narrowly just about ourselves when making decisions, and instead consider more of the consequences. This will feed into how we practise the other limbs of the path, and conversely our practice of the other limbs will help us to view ourselves, others, and the world more accurately.

Right intention

Right intention involves living our lives in accordance with positive values, such as appreciation, goodwill, compassion, equanimity, confidence in one's potential and that of others, and contentment. Intention is crucial. I have found that, when I do a kind deed because I want someone to like me, the consequences are very different from when I do it with an open heart. This limb emphasizes that the attitude underlying what we do to practise the other limbs is fundamentally important.

Practice

At the end of each day, bring to mind anything anyone has done for you during the day, and spend a minute appreciating them and what they have done. It can be something small, such as saying 'hello', or a bit bigger, such as cooking some food for you, or driving a bus you caught, or looking after a garden you enjoyed.

Right speech

It is interesting that speech is considered so important that it's given a limb of its own. There are four aspects to right speech, which are:

- being truthful;
- being kind;
- being helpful;
- and promoting harmony.

Truthful speech will be explored in more detail in the next chapter. I'll just make a few points about the other aspects of right speech. The first is that these aspects need to be applied to our internal speech – the way we talk to ourselves – as well as to the way we talk to others. Many of us can be rather judgemental and critical in the way we talk to ourselves. It can be hard to silence the inner critic. You may find it helpful to reflect on whether you would speak to a friend in this way and to try to talk to yourself more kindly. You may want to remind yourself that you are doing your best and that being human is difficult sometimes.

Being helpful does not mean giving advice, however well-intentioned that advice may be. It is often more helpful to simply listen carefully and kindly, and to be interested and ask questions in order to understand better.

My favourite way of promoting harmony is to notice when someone says something complimentary about someone else and to tell the person being praised what this person has said.

Practice

Notice whether your internal speech is truthful and kind.

Find a way to practise kindly speech, helpful speech, or speech that promotes harmony.

Right action

This limb is concerned about ethical action. Practising it helps us to become more like an enlightened being. This limb is explored in detail in the next chapter.

Right livelihood

Work takes much of our time and energy, so what work we do is important. We want to avoid work that does harm. The Buddha advised against dealing in weapons of war, trafficking in living beings, and selling drink or drugs. You can probably think of other occupations it would be good to avoid. If you feel uneasy about what you do, it may not be straightforward to change it, so finding a more suitable job may become a long-term goal. Ideally, work supports the values you have.

Reflection

In what ways does your work support your values, and in what ways do you feel uncomfortable about what you are being asked to do or how you are being expected to behave?

Right effort

Right effort involves developing and maintaining skilful mental states – in particular generosity, love, and wisdom – and preventing or eradicating unskilful mental states, in particular craving, hatred, and delusion. A good place to start is maintaining the positive mental states we have already and cultivating them further. It can't be done by force. I've recently watched some programmes following the UK ambulance service. It has impressed me how they look after each other, give everyone the time they need, and speak so positively and kindly about everyone they help. It inspires me to be a little more like them, so watching the programmes helps me to cultivate more positive states of mind.

It is easier to prevent unskilful mental states than to eradicate them once they have arisen. I also notice that the news can bring about unskilful mental states, particularly of anxiety, so I limit how much I look at it. The times when I want to look at the news many times a day are those when it is likely to be most helpful to avoid it, or at least limit it.

Reflection

What helps you to have a more skilful state of mind?

What tends to bring an unskilful state of mind?

Right mindfulness

Mindfulness has a lot of aspects. We can be mindful of many different parts of our experience, including the body, our feelings, and our thoughts. To start, it is good just to focus on what is going on in the body. The body can be very rich with sensations, and you will notice more as you become more practised. As we go about our day, it is easy to ignore the body except when it is rather uncomfortable. Just from a very practical point of view, it can be helpful simply to notice how we are sitting and standing, and to notice how awareness can lead us naturally to alter our posture. As you become more aware of the sensations in the body, you may notice how emotions can be felt there.

Being mindful is about being present in experience, rather than thinking about it. We'll do a short activity to explore this.

Activity

Start by looking at your hands, and you may notice various things about them such as lines on the palms, blood vessels under the skin, and so on. You can describe the hands to yourself.

Now bring awareness into your hands and shake them. Notice the sensations of movement. Touch various surfaces and notice the different sensations of touch, of warmth and coolness, of rough and smooth. Lastly, let the hand be still, and discover what sensations there are of touch and temperature and maybe tingling.

How was thinking about your hands different from bringing awareness into them and experiencing the sensations? It is this latter experience that is what is meant by mindfulness.

In the context of the eightfold path, mindfulness, the attitude we bring to our awareness, also matters. It is helpful to:

- make a balanced effort, where you keep letting the object of your awareness take centre stage, but without straining;
- allow your experience to be as it is without judgement and without trying to change it;
- bring kindness, for example gently breathing into any discomfort and softening around it as best you can;
- remember your higher purpose and the value of the practice you are doing;
- take an interest and explore, for example noticing the boundaries of any sensation in the body and how experiences arise and pass away.

The following practice brings mindfulness to the different sensations in the body and then to the body as a whole. It's a helpful practice to do regularly, and you are likely to find that it feels different on different days and that your experience changes over time. It's a good idea to make yourself as comfortable as you can before doing this practice. You can either sit or lie down.

Practice: mindful body scan (fifteen minutes)

If you wish, you can follow this link: https://tinyurl.com/SotBP-audio, or read through these instructions and follow them as best you can:

- You can do the practice either sitting upright in a chair or lying down, in a way that is both relaxed and alert. You can close your eyes or keep them open if there is a danger that you will fall asleep.
- Take time to tune in to a sense of the whole body. Perhaps getting a sense of the contact with what you are sitting or lying on, a sense of temperature, and gradually tuning in to a sense of the body and how you are sitting or lying.
- Then gathering your attention and allowing it to settle on the sensations of breathing, so maybe having a sense

of the movement of air in your nostrils, throat, chest, or abdominal area. If it's helpful, take a couple of more deliberate breaths, perhaps becoming aware of the rising of chest and abdomen on each inbreath and the release on each outbreath.

- You're not trying to achieve any particular state or even relax. Instead, just becoming aware of experience, however it is.
- Now letting the sensations of breathing be in the background as you systematically direct your attention to different parts of the body.
- First bringing awareness into your toes and feet. Becoming aware of any sensations throughout both feet. Perhaps you can feel the contact of the floor and with clothing, or some tingling or numbness, sensations on the surface or deeper into the body of the feet. If there are no sensations, just being aware of that absence.
- Then taking a more intentional inbreath into the feet, and on the outbreath letting go of the feet and bringing awareness into your legs.
- Then letting go of the legs and bringing awareness into the torso, starting with the contact of the buttocks with seat or floor and expanding to include the whole of the back.
- From time to time, you will find that your attention is distracted and pulled away from the body. This isn't a mistake or failure, it's what minds sometimes do. When you notice, simply acknowledge what you are experiencing in this moment, and gently bring attention back to the sensations in the back.
- Now moving to the abdomen and its gentle rise and fall with the breath, then feeling the expansion and contraction of the ribs.
- Then letting go of awareness of the torso and bringing the spotlight of your awareness into the hands, then the arms.

- Then bringing the focus of awareness to the neck, then face and scalp.
- Then broadening awareness to have a sense of the whole body.
- Lastly, simply sitting or lying here.

There are other senses too that we can bring mindfulness to, such as hearing, taste, and smell. Mindfulness is something you can explore throughout the day, when brushing teeth, when drinking a cup of tea or coffee, and when standing waiting in a queue.

Practice

Choose an activity you do every day, such as brushing your teeth, drinking a cup of tea, cooking, or taking the dog for a walk. See if you can be more awake or present in it by becoming more aware of the sensations in the body as you do it. You will probably find that your mind keeps getting caught up in thoughts. That is natural. Noticing that this is happening is also a part of mindfulness, so congratulate yourself for noticing, and then allow the sensations in the body to take centre stage again.

It can be hard to remember to be mindful, so it can help to do something like tie a piece of string around your toothbrush to remind you. After focusing on one activity for a week, you may like to change to a different one.

Right meditation

This limb is sometimes translated as concentration, but that may not be the most helpful way to think about it. In meditation, we are aiming for some degree of:

- awareness of the whole body;
- kindness, being non-judgemental, having a sense of well-being;
- openness to and interest in what is happening in experience;
- savouring and enjoyment of what is pleasurable without clinging on to it;
- clarity in the mind.

It is easier to develop these qualities if we have a relatively uncluttered mind. These days, that can be difficult as the internet can be very beguiling and we are surrounded by social media. I find that it helps to go for walks in nature or spend time in a garden, and to limit how much I look at my devices.

In our everyday lives, it helps to have a daily meditation practice, even if it is only ten minutes a day. I have spent many years meditating for forty or fifty minutes a day and it has really borne fruit, both in how I experience my life and in how my mind is able to calm much more fully when I go on retreat. There is also much that we can put in place in our lives that is helpful, such as having enough sleep, taking walks in nature, noticing beauty, and cultivating appreciation and gratitude.

Practice

Try taking up a meditation practice for at least a week and ideally a month, and notice the effect it has. It can be hard learning to meditate from a book, and I suggest going to the website https://www.wildmind.org, where there are meditation courses available to teach you to meditate. There are more suggestions for learning to meditate in chapter 8. You could start with mindfulness of breathing and then follow your interest.

4 Morality

The Buddha emphasized that what he was teaching was dukkha (suffering) and the cessation of dukkha (the way to reduce suffering). One of the most straightforward ways to reduce suffering for ourselves and for others is to act more ethically. In this chapter, we shall explore how to do this.

In the last chapter, we explored most of the noble eightfold path, which provides a way to end dukkha. In this chapter, we shall explore right action. Together with right speech and right livelihood, right action forms a practical way to move towards becoming the person you would like to be and to reduce dukkha. They are all about how to behave more ethically.

How can we decide what is a right action? It can be helpful to keep in mind that right action should be considered not solely by itself, but in conjunction with the other limbs of the eightfold path. So for example:

- The **view** behind the action is relevant. If we were to understand our place in the world more accurately, then there is no way that we would want to harm others or distort the truth because we would see the consequences of doing so.
- Right **intention** and right **effort** involve encouraging skilful mental states based on generosity, love, and wisdom. These mental states support us in acting ethically in a more wholehearted way and bring peace of mind.

To help us know how to act, the Buddha gave precepts, which are guidelines of ways to behave in order to progress towards transcending suffering. There are five precepts that are followed by all Buddhists, which we shall explore in this chapter. You are already practising these precepts every time you say a kind word, or give someone a present, or speak the truth.

It may seem that practising the precepts is a straightforward way to make progress on the path towards Enlightenment. However, it is more subtle than it first appears. In reflecting on what to say in this chapter, I became increasingly aware that what might be useful for one person might not be for someone else. Our underlying tendencies and the conditions we are in make a lot of difference. Let's first explore two different emphases in acting more ethically, and then we can look at how different approaches can be helpful for different people.

There are two aspects to being more ethical: our actions and the state of mind in which we do them. We shall explore both in detail later in the chapter. Now we shall take an overview. When we follow the precepts, it affects our way of being in the world and sets up good habits, so the precepts are often referred to as training principles. When we explore our states of mind, we find that they can be divided into those that are skilful or helpful and those that are unskilful or unhelpful. Skilful mental states are those that are imbued with generosity, love, and wisdom, while states of mind coloured by greed, hatred, and delusion are unskilful. These aspects of following the precepts and developing skilful states of mind are both important and support each other.

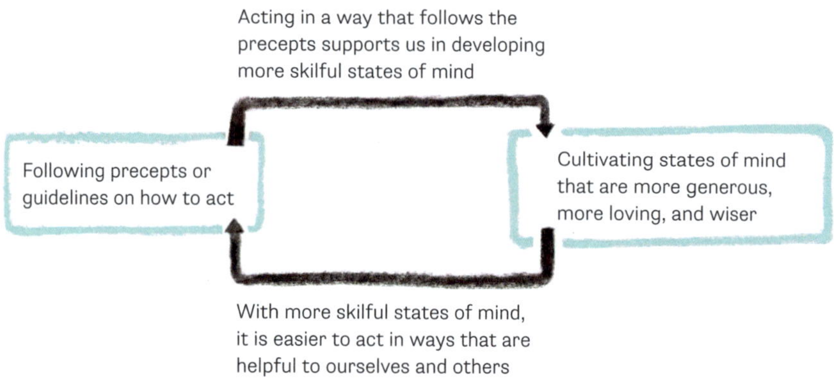

Practising morality in these ways is an indispensable foundation for progress on the path. When we behave more ethically, we have less to regret, so meditation becomes more enjoyable and we can go deeper. One of my favourite teachings of the Buddha starts like this, and then goes on to give various stages that naturally follow, ending in liberation:

> For a virtuous person, one whose behaviour is virtuous, no volition need be exerted: 'Let non-regret arise in me.' It is natural that non-regret arises in one who is virtuous, one whose behaviour is virtuous.
>
> For one without regret no volition need be exerted: 'Let joy arise in me.' It is natural that joy arises in one without regret.[31]

The following table outlines some of the advantages of each approach and how they support each other. You may be able to add to the table as we progress through the chapter.

Why it can be helpful to have ethical guidelines to follow	**Why it can be helpful to develop skilful states of mind**
We may find it hard to be aware of our state of mind.	The mode of mind in which we do an action makes a difference to the outcome.
It can be hard to imagine ourselves in a different state of mind and to bring a change about. Simply doing a skilful action can help bring about that change.	We can take our practice deeper by examining our state of mind as we act according to the precepts.
Because the precepts are concerned with action in the world, focusing on them counteracts any tendency to be solely concerned with our own mental state.	Treating the precepts as rules that must be followed can lead to a judgemental state of mind and ill will towards anyone who acts otherwise. Cultivating well-wishing can bring more love and compassion.

Which approach is more helpful for you to emphasize at the moment depends on many factors. It is different for different people and depends on your tendencies and the conditions you are in. Below are some examples I noticed when teaching.

Some people have very busy lives and can be out of touch with how they feel. They also lack the time and space to reflect on how their actions affect others. For such people, guidelines on how to act can be invaluable.

Some people have many caring duties, so the emphasis in their lives is looking after others. This can be very generous behaviour, and outwardly such people can be very ethical in their actions. The danger is that they can ignore their own needs. So such people might become very tired or feel some resentment. These feelings can fester in the shadows and affect *how* they act. Such people need more awareness of their own mental states, honesty and openness with themselves and others, and to realize that their well-being matters too.

Many people are very critical of themselves. People dwell on what they perceive as their failures more than their successes. Such people often think in terms of 'should' or 'ought', so can be very judgemental of what they are thinking or doing. They have a view that they are not good enough. For such people, a list of guidelines on how to behave can just add to their judgements about themselves. For them, it is important to become kinder to themselves and more aware of the ways in which they are already following the precepts. In this way, they can have a more balanced view of themselves.

Other people act in ways that they think will make them happier, but actually bring more distress after the immediate gratification. Examples include regularly drinking alcohol, vaping, shopping for the pleasure of acquiring new things, being obsessed with social media, gambling. These are all potentially addictive behaviours and can be hard to change. For these people, it can be helpful to focus on any behaviours that reduce the harm. So it can be helpful for them to spend time with different people, to occupy themselves with doing something more positive, or to bring more awareness to how they feel when doing what they tend to do.

Reflection

What are your tendencies around morality? When do you think that an emphasis on guidelines might be helpful for you, and when would an emphasis on state of mind be helpful?

We'll next look in detail at the precepts, and then we'll explore how to cultivate more skilful mental states.

The precepts

The Buddha taught the precepts as guidelines for how to behave. They are principles rather than rules, so we need to think about how to put them into practice. They are more like a direction than a destination.

The five precepts below are followed by all Buddhists. Traditionally they are given as things to avoid, but I find it more helpful to look at the positive versions we use in the Triratna Community I belong to, as they make the direction of change clearer:

Traditional precepts	**Positive precepts**
I undertake to abstain from harming living beings.	With deeds of loving-kindness, I purify my body.
I undertake to abstain from taking the not-given.	With open-handed generosity, I purify my body.
I undertake to abstain from sexual misconduct.	With stillness, simplicity, and contentment, I purify my body.
I undertake to abstain from false speech.	With truthful communication, I purify my speech.
I undertake to abstain from taking intoxicants.	With mindfulness clear and radiant, I purify my mind.

Let's look at each precept in turn to explore what is meant.

Abstaining from harming living beings/developing kindness

Harming people or animals is an unwholesome and unskilful act because it betrays the fundamental fellowship of all living beings. Harming others can have widespread repercussions.

Most Buddhists practise this precept by eating a vegetarian diet. What pushed me to become vegetarian was hearing that people who worked in slaughterhouses were badly affected by what they had to do. Since then, I have gradually become vegan, as I have become more concerned about the way animals are treated in the food industry. It was not easy to give up cheese, and it does require some care to ensure that I have all the nutrients I need. The benefits are appreciating the flavours of plants more and feeling lighter in my heart.

I'm aware that not everyone finds it easy to be vegetarian or vegan because of their particular health issues. It's not straightforward or sensible for everyone. Also, I'm fortunate to have a husband who shares my values about not harming animals so my social context is supportive. It may be more difficult for you.

This precept includes kindness to ourselves as well as to others. In our minds, we can tend to focus on what we have done that we don't like. Then it is easy in our internal talk to speak quite unkindly to ourselves, in a way that we wouldn't dream of talking to a friend. However, that unkindness to ourselves is unhelpful. It is much better to notice what we do that we are pleased about, as that encourages us to repeat the behaviour. So notice the times when you speak kindly to someone, or hold a door open for them, or spend time with someone who is lonely, or send a message thanking someone, or pick up some rubbish, or give a small gift, or...

Kindness to ourselves does not mean indulgence in habits that are unhealthy. It is about looking after our bodies and minds as well as we can. On a straightforward level, being kind to ourselves involves self-care, such as taking some exercise regularly, without overdoing it, eating healthily, spending time in nature, listening to uplifting music, connecting with others, and taking enough rest and sleep. Taking it further, it can also involve setting boundaries, especially when someone is being demanding of your time or energy; being more courageous about expressing or living out what is most important to you; preventing others from being harmed; taking on feedback from others; and doing what you believe it is right to do even if you don't want to. By being kind to yourself in these ways, it is easier to be kind to others with an open heart.

The obvious ways to practise this precept are to avoid harming others either physically or mentally. In case you need more ideas, here is a list of possibilities. You are probably doing some of these things already, and maybe some are simply too difficult at the moment. I encourage you to choose a suggestion that involves a little effort. If there is nothing here that suits you, then add your own ideas that are relevant to you.

Practice

- Be more patient with your children for a day.
- Be vegetarian (or vegan) for a day, or a day a week.
- Pick up a piece of rubbish from the street and recycle it if you can.
- Say thank you and mean it.
- Eat a bit more healthily.
- Give yourself permission to be human when noticing how you are feeling.
- Spend twenty minutes doing something that raises your spirits.
- Make a note of something you have done that you are pleased about.

- Ask someone how they are and be interested in the answer.
- Avoid losing your temper and shouting at someone.

The following quote is a lovely summary of what it means to follow this precept:

> That best portion of a good man's life
> His little, nameless, unremembered, acts
> Of kindness and of love.[32]

Abstaining from taking the not-given/generosity

Not taking the not-given is a stronger practice than not stealing. It means that we should not avoid taxes, take items from work without permission, or keep money that we have found in the street. It can also include taking someone's time or energy when they don't want to give it.

By contrast, generosity is a powerful practice as it counteracts our tendency to focus on ourselves and acquisition. Open-hearted generosity is a great blessing to those around us. It encourages us to take others into account. This broader concern brings wisdom, as it reflects a more realistic view of the world. The world does not revolve around us, however much we want it to.

It is easy to assume that generosity involves giving money or material things, but there are many ways in which we can be generous. Some other ways described in the Buddhist tradition are:

- giving time and energy to others;
- thinking of ways to benefit others (I've found it shocking how many of my thoughts are about me);
- giving of knowledge, art, and culture;

- giving of fearlessness, since you can reassure people by your presence;
- giving of life and limb;
- giving the gift of the Dharma.

How you give is also important. Here is some advice from the Buddha:

> There are these five gifts of a good person. What five? They give a gift out of faith; they give a gift respectfully; they give a timely gift; they give a gift unreservedly; they give a gift without injuring themselves or others.[33]

The gift of the Dharma is the greatest gift you can give, as it helps relieve the basis of suffering. The Buddha showed the depth of his compassion by teaching, and so helping others both immediately and down the generations. If you practise wholeheartedly, even in a small way, it makes a difference not just to you, but to everyone you meet, and that difference extends out much further than you can imagine. Most of us underestimate the impact we have on others.

In our society, there is a culture of getting value for money. This acts against generosity. The way I was caught up in that tendency came home to me quite strongly when I found a book I liked in an Oxfam shop, but was reluctant to buy it because it was priced at £20, which seemed expensive for what it was. Then I realized that I would be quite happy to give Oxfam £20, so why was I hesitating? I gave the shop assistant £20 and they gave me the book. The transaction felt quite different from usual. I found that the attitude could naturally be carried over to payments to individuals or organizations where I had a sense of gratitude or appreciation for their values. Making a payment then became more heart-opening.

Many institutions in Triratna, the Buddhist movement I belong to, are based on generosity. So people are not paid to teach, and volunteers do many of the support tasks. When people attend courses or events, they pay what they can afford, rather than a fixed price. This way of running activities relies on everyone having a vision of helping others and of creating a community.

Practice

Here are some ideas for how to practise this precept. You may like to add some ideas of your own.

- Share a meal with someone.
- Reduce waste by recycling or reusing.
- Share your enthusiasm for something you find beautiful.
- Walk or cycle rather than driving one day.
- Give someone some time and space by listening to them.
- Allow someone out in front of you either when driving a car or when leaving a train or bus.
- Spend ten minutes reflecting on how you might make someone's life happier.
- Give some money to charity.
- Arrive on time when you have arranged to meet someone.

Abstaining from sexual misconduct/developing stillness, simplicity, and contentment

Sexual misconduct means acting without respect for others, for example having sex with other people's spouses or partners, which can cause tremendous pain, or forcing sexual advances on someone without their consent. So this precept is about treating others with love and respect, and considering the consequences of our actions.

Buddhists in the modern world generally have no problem with homosexuality or with sexual activity, as long as it's based on respect and care. However, our emotions in sexual and romantic relationships can be very strong, and this can make acting skilfully in this area challenging. This is especially true since it can be difficult to take on board the wishes of one's sexual partner when one's partner may change their mind.

This precept can be interpreted more broadly as avoiding misconduct by craving stimulation, intensity, and excitement. For example, I've noticed the temptation of searching the internet for something to buy, so that I can have a little burst of excitement from ordering it. By the time the article arrives, that excitement has waned and I may hardly care about it, and I might realize that I have wasted money.

There isn't a problem about desire and enjoyment as long as you can avoid being fixated on a particular outcome. There is a lovely story about the Dalai Lama visiting a monastery where they made cheese and cake. Afterwards, he talked about the visit on the radio and said that at the monastery they gave him some cheese and what he really wanted was cake. Then he burst into laughter. What a wonderful way to respond to not getting what you want.

The problems come when we want something to give us more than it is able to give, for example, wanting cake to distract us from feeling stressed. We can find it easier to accept happily whatever happens if we can increase our feelings of contentment. Deliberately noticing what is good in our experience can help with this.

Practice

Ideas for ways to practise this precept include the following. Again, please feel free to add ideas of your own.

- Meditate.
- Do something that feeds your mind, such as listening to music you find beautiful, looking at some art you enjoy, or simply sitting quietly.

- Eat more frugally for a day.
- Spend some time outside enjoying nature.
- Notice any times you spend daydreaming about someone you find attractive, and notice the effect it has.
- At the end of the day, make a note of anything good that happened.
- Ask your sexual partner, if you have one, what they like and don't like you to do.
- Avoid browsing on Amazon and other shopping sites.
- Don't follow the news for a day, and notice what effect that has on your mind.
- Have a day without looking at social media.

Abstaining from false speech/being truthful

There are two aspects of truthful speech. The first is being factually truthful. We often bend the truth by exaggerating or minimizing. This needs watching in internal speech too. As well as being untrue, it can be unhelpful to have thoughts such as 'I'll *always* feel like this' or 'I shouldn't *ever* make mistakes.' It's more truthful and kinder to say to yourself, 'I'm feeling like this now, but it will probably feel different tomorrow/next week' or 'It's normal to make mistakes sometimes.'

The second aspect is being truthful about what we are thinking and feeling. This can be challenging because we may not know what we are thinking and feeling, because it can challenge our sense of identity to see and admit to what we really think and feel, and also because we may be afraid of upsetting other people or concerned about what they may think of us. Of course, speaking this truth needs to be done with care. This is the Buddha's advice in these circumstances:

If you know anything that is hurtful and untrue, don't say it.
If you know anything that is helpful and untrue, don't say it.
If you know anything that is hurtful and true, don't say it.
If you know anything that is helpful and true, find the right time.[34]

Being open about our experience can sometimes be surprisingly beneficial. A friend of mine belongs to a small group of Buddhists who meet regularly to support each other in their practice. During one of their meetings, she noticed that she was feeling bored. She said how she felt in a kindly way, and encouraged the others in the group to be equally open and honest. The result was very beneficial for everyone. As they became more open with each other about themselves, they started to both enjoy their meetings and appreciate each other more.

Practice

Here are some ideas for practising this precept of telling the truth.

- Be honest in business dealings as far as you are able.
- Be frank, in a way that's kind and useful, when talking to a friend.
- Be more truthful with yourself about how you are feeling.
- With a lot of kindness and gentleness, notice when you deviate from truthful speech, why you did, and how it feels.
- When you notice yourself exaggerating or minimizing when telling someone what has happened to you, rephrase so that it is more accurate, at least in your mind if it's too late to do out loud.
- As best you can, don't overgeneralize: 'This is difficult – everything's such an effort.'
- Avoid gossip if you can, or ensure that it is kind.

Abstaining from intoxicants/becoming more mindful

Traditionally the fifth precept is understood to mean abstinence from drinking alcohol. I found that, when I started to meditate, drinking alcohol became less attractive because I noticed how, when I had a drink, my mind felt as if it were in a fog. The fog felt very unpleasant, so I naturally stopped wanting to drink alcohol. This doesn't happen to everyone, so it may be harder for you. I still enjoy alcoholic chocolates, so the abstinence is not absolute.

We can be intoxicated in other ways too, such as when we occupy our minds with something that numbs it, such as watching mindless TV. This can bring some relief from stress and pain, but it also deadens the mind. So it can diminish our ability to enjoy beauty and other people.

Activity

In this context, it can be helpful to notice your mood or emotional state, and how it's affected by what you do. See if you can build up a list of activities that nourish you or make you feel more alive. You might try going out for a short walk, or reading something pleasurable, or meeting a friend, or doing some housework, or...

Practice

Here are some short mindfulness practices that you can build into your day. You may like to add ideas that are more relevant to you.

- While waiting for a kettle to boil, bring awareness to the sensations in your feet, legs, arms, and hands.
- Be more aware of the body when going up or down stairs.

- Focus on eating one mouthful of food without doing anything else at the same time, and become more aware of taste.
- Observe the effect something has on you, for example reading the paper or watching a particular TV programme. Is there any tension in the body?
- Be mindful of the sensations of breathing for three breaths.
- Have a month without alcohol.
- When listening to someone, be more mindful of them rather than of what you want to say next.
- Bring awareness to your posture as you sit at a computer.
- Keep a mood diary – in a small notebook, write time and date and mood as many times as possible for a day or a week.
- When you are tempted to do whatever you tend to do when experience is difficult, try something from your list of nourishing or enlivening activities. What happens?

Cultivating more skilful states of mind

Now that we have explored the precepts, let's move to the other aspect of morality: our state of mind. When starting an ethical practice, it can be helpful to focus on overt actions. As our actions become more ethical, we can focus more on thoughts and our underlying attitude. These states of mind are very significant.

When I started on the Buddhist path, I was surprised to find that just wishing someone well, even without seeing them, could improve the quality of our connection when we next met. Even so, just having a thought that it would be good to give someone a present is not nearly as powerful as actually giving the present.

This is how the Buddha describes the importance of what happens in our minds:

> Experiences are preceded by mind, led by mind, and produced by mind. If one speaks or acts with an impure mind, suffering follows even as the cartwheel follows the hoof of the ox.
>
> Experiences are preceded by mind, led by mind, and produced by mind. If one speaks or acts with a pure mind, happiness follows like a shadow that never departs.[35]

An impure mind is one based on the unskilful states of craving, ill will, and spiritual ignorance; a pure mind is one based on the skilful states of generosity, compassion, and understanding.

It's a helpful practice to examine your own experience. I find that, when I'm obsessed with getting my own way, or I'm letting annoyance dictate my behaviour, then I feel contracted and it's unpleasant. When I'm generous or kind to someone, I feel lighter and more spacious. Regular meditation helps us to be more aware of these feelings when they arise.

Reflection: how does it feel to be more ethical?

Recollect some time when you acted meanly or unkindly. How did that feel? Then recollect a time when you were generous or kind. How did that feel?

As a first step in cultivating more skilful states of mind, it is helpful simply to be aware of our mode of mind and the effect it has. The Buddha discovered this as part of his path towards Enlightenment. Before he was enlightened, the Buddha-to-be noticed that thoughts of sensual desire, ill will, and cruelty led to unhappiness for him and others, while thoughts of renunciation, loving-kindness, and compassion aided wisdom and did not cause difficulties.[36] He used this observation to help him abandon thoughts of sensual desire, ill will, and cruelty, and to encourage thoughts of renunciation, loving-kindness, and compassion.

It can be a challenging practice to observe your state of mind. For example, I've found that there can be feelings of shame when I notice anger, because I like to think of myself as a calm and kind person. I need to remind myself that it's not my fault that there is anger, and that I'm being skilful by noticing it. Being aware gives me more choices about what to do, and helps me to act more skilfully.

We can do something similar to the Buddha by looking at a slightly simpler division of modes of mind in more modern language. There are three major types of our emotion-regulation systems as described by Professor Paul Gilbert,[37] and we shall give each of them a colour:

- safety-seeking, involving emotions such as anxiety, anger, and disgust - red mode;
- resource-seeking, involving grasping, achieving, consuming - blue mode;
- contentment and connection, involving affection and kindness, being happy with the way things are, and a sense of well-being - green mode.

These modes interact with each other.

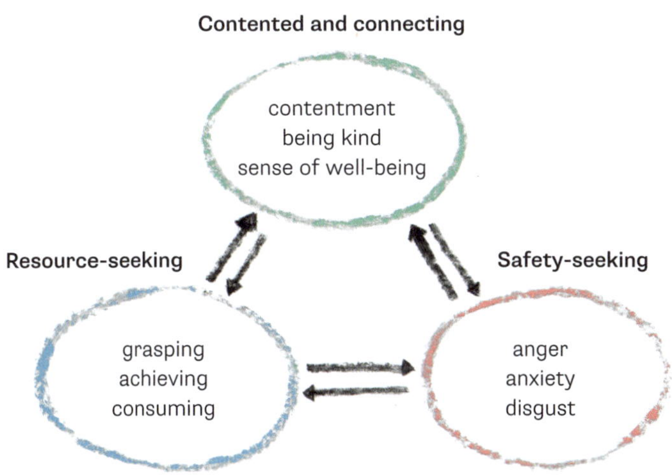

Practice

Spend a minute noticing whether your mode of mind is predominantly red (safety-seeking), predominantly blue (resource-seeking), or predominantly green (contented and connecting).

Notice what effect your mode of mind has on how you act (the consequences for others).

This practice of noticing the mode of mind and its consequences is developing our skilfulness in what we do and how we do it. It takes courage, persistence, and attitudes of exploration and kindness. It can be helpful to compare it to the skilfulness needed to play the piano. We don't get better at playing the piano just by thinking about it, nor by being terrified of making a mistake. We improve at playing the piano, and at becoming more moral, through practice and learning from outcomes.

We can also set up conditions that will encourage skilful mental states. Here is a meditation you can try which should take about ten minutes. It can be particularly helpful if you tend towards being self-critical.

Practice

Start by sitting comfortably and with dignity.

Then bring to mind a friend or acquaintance you like or appreciate. For a few minutes, reflect on the qualities they have that you appreciate.

Then, for a minute or two, reflect on how this friend or acquaintance isn't perfect, but they are doing their best.

Lastly, bring to mind how you too, like this friend, have values, and how you do your best to live by them.

Karma

To finish, let's examine the topic of karma. The law of karma is quite often misunderstood. A simple description of its meaning in Buddhism is that actions have consequences. That is, what we think, what we say, and what we do make a difference to our mind, to our relationships with others, and to what happens in our lives. We can change what we think, say, and do. If we make these changes in a positive way, it will have a positive effect on our lives. This is not just a Buddhist idea, as you can tell from the following quotations. The first one is a saying that has been attributed to several different people:

> Sow a thought and you reap an action; sow an act and you reap a habit; sow a habit and you reap a character; sow a character and you reap a destiny.

> Moral virtues come from habit. [...] They are in us neither by nature, nor in despite of nature, but we are furnished by nature with a capacity for receiving them, and we develop them through habit. [...] These virtues we acquire by first exercising them, as in the case of other arts. Whatever we learn to do, we learn by actually doing it: men come to be builders, for instance, by building, and harp players, by playing the harp. In the same way, by doing just acts we come to be just; by doing self-controlled acts, we come to be self-controlled; and by doing brave acts, we come to be brave.[38]

Karma rests on two assumptions: human character is malleable, so we can all change; and volitional actions (actions we choose to make) modify character, so provide the path to change. As we have seen, the Buddha claimed that actions based on skilful states of mind would bring happiness, while those based on unskilful states of mind would bring suffering.

Just making a small difference to our habits can eventually have an effect. I've found that reading something uplifting, rather than looking at the news, while drinking my early morning cup of tea, makes a difference to my state of mind for much of the morning.

The effect is magnified after making the change for several days on the trot. This is how the Buddha puts it:

Do not underestimate good,
thinking, 'It will not approach me.'
A water-pot becomes full by the
constant falling of drops of water.
Similarly, the wise person little by
little fills themselves with good.[39]

Reflection

Is there a small action that you could do that might make a difference to your mind if done repeatedly?

What difference would it make to others and the world if you made a small change to your state of mind?

Let's finish this chapter with a quotation from the Buddha:

> Wisdom is purified by morality, and morality is purified by wisdom: where one is, the other is, the moral person has wisdom and the wise person has morality, and the combination of morality and wisdom is called the highest thing in the world.[40]

5 The Buddhist Community

We've met the idea that practising Buddhism involves the Buddha, Dharma, and Sangha. In chapter 2, we explored the Buddha as an ideal, and in chapters 3 and 4 we explored the teachings and practices that Buddhists follow. Now we shall investigate sangha, the spiritual community. We shall do this by firstly looking at why sangha is important, then I'll give a brief summary of the major schools of Buddhism to show the variety of Buddhist communities. Lastly, I'll describe my experience to show what it can be like to become involved in one of the recent schools of Buddhism that have developed over the last century.

The importance of sangha

So why is sangha important? Human beings are very social. What other people think is important to us. For example, there can be a strong desire to wear clothes that will fit in and be acceptable to others, particularly when going to a football match or out to a party. It is hard to avoid acting in similar ways to our friends or people we are with.

So the company we keep can make a lot of difference to our practice. One Tibetan Buddhist teacher talks about how being with true spiritual friends and following their example will naturally imbue you with their good qualities, just as all the birds flying around a golden mountain are bathed in its golden radiance. It's certainly true that I have experienced that feeling of being in a golden glow when with people with a strong practice. Although being with strong practitioners is particularly valuable, I find that all connections with others can be valuable: not just for the opportunity to share experiences, but also because I can learn from anyone, even those who are relatively new to practice, since they may ask questions that challenge my habitual ways of thinking, or may articulate their experience more eloquently than I can do.

Reflection

Reflect on times when you have been influenced by others, either to behave better than you might otherwise have done, or to behave worse.

The Buddha clearly valued spiritual friendship, as this story shows:

> The Venerable Ananda approached the Blessed One, paid homage to him, sat down to one side and said:
>
> 'Venerable sir, this is half of the spiritual life, that is, good friendship, good companionship, good comradeship.'
>
> 'Not so, Ananda! Not so, Ananda! This is the entire spiritual life, Ananda, that is good friendship, good companionship, good comradeship. When a disciple has a good friend, a good companion, a good comrade, it is to be expected that they will develop and cultivate the Noble Eightfold Path.'[41]

Traditionally, the sangha refuge or support is about being with people who are experienced and strong practitioners. This Arya Sangha, literally 'noble community,' consists of those experienced and strong practitioners who have had some form of spiritual insight. It may be hard to find such people, but you shouldn't despair, because there are ways in which people only just ahead of us can be most helpful.

When we start on the Buddhist path, it's an effort to practise. We may meditate for a while, or avoid getting drunk, but then decide that it's too much effort to keep it up. It can be so helpful to meet people who are meditating regularly and don't drink, and yet seem contented and very much alive and engaged. I remember being fascinated by the different perspective experienced Buddhists had on my life, and touched by their interest in me.

Sometimes they saw the good in me that I had difficulty seeing myself. Also, it felt such a relief to find people who shared my values and wanted to talk about things that matter.

Those who have irreversible insight are called stream entrants, because they have entered a stream that pulls them along. Practice is no longer the effort it is when you start. Stream entrants have broken three fetters, three ways of being that can hold us back. These fetters are:

- **personality view**, believing oneself to be fixed and unchanging, that we cannot change the way we are;
- **dependence on moral rules and religious observances as ends in themselves**, for example, following the ethical precepts because you want people to like you;
- **doubt**, an inability to make up one's mind and commit oneself and put one's heart into what one does.

Another way of thinking about these fetters is that they involve being bound by habits, acting for appearances rather than wholeheartedly, and being vague or undecided. Overcoming these tendencies takes time and effort.

One difficulty with taking refuge in the Arya Sangha is finding people who are or close to becoming stream entrants. It's likely to be difficult to recognize them even if you do find one. So, in the beginning, it is helpful simply to find others who are also wanting to follow the Buddhist path. This is the maha-sangha, the 'great sangha,' which consists of all those who regard themselves as Buddhist or who are doing Buddhist practices in some way or other. You can connect with this sangha via books and talks, but it is even better to meet people in person if you can, either in a Buddhist group or on retreat.

I shall have some more to say about connecting with other Buddhists later. We shall now go through a brief summary of the history of Buddhism, and take a brief look at the main schools. The aim is to show the variety of approaches and to give a flavour of each school. Different schools can appeal and be helpful to different temperaments. So, as we go through, I invite you to notice the effect on you of each of the teachings we shall meet. To finish the chapter, we shall explore the Buddhist community that I belong to as an example of a modern Buddhist movement. It can illustrate the sorts of relationships with other Buddhists that are helpful.

A brief history of Buddhism and its schools

Early Buddhism

Soon after the Buddha's death, probably around 400 BCE, the first Buddhist communal recitation was held to collect and preserve the Buddha's teachings. These teachings were then passed down orally for many hundreds of years before being written down. The teachings were collected into various canonical collections. All except one, the Pali Canon, were subsequently lost, although some are preserved in Chinese translation, and many further fragments survive in Sanskrit and other languages.

Buddhism remained a fairly minor religion until King Ashoka converted in about 260 BCE. He spread Buddhism far beyond the confines of India, both south to Sri Lanka and west as far as Greece.

The Pali Canon has been preserved in the Theravadin school. The name of the school means 'Teachings of the Elders'. It has an emphasis on ethics, monastic lineage, and discipline. There have been some changes since the Buddha's time. In particular, the Buddha ordained women as well as men, but, after the Buddha's death, the ordination of women died out in Theravadin countries, although it was maintained in China.

The goal in the Theravadin school is the achievement of the state of Arahant ('worthy one', 'winner of Nirvana'), which is a state of Enlightenment where rebirth is ended. The community consists of monks (who, in theory, practise full time, meditate, and teach) and lay people (whose practice mostly consists of ethics and providing for the monks). Lay people aim to build up merit, which is like a store of goodness. The Theravadins believe that this merit allows them to have a better life when they are reborn.

Theravada has for many centuries been the predominant religion of Sri Lanka and continental South-East Asia. Buddhism died out in India almost entirely by the end of the twelfth century CE as Hinduism took over, although there has been a revival recently.

We have met many teachings from the Pali Canon already. They emphasize ethics and how to work with our minds. This can be done via stories and also straightforwardly, as here:

> Those who entertain such thoughts as 'He abused me, he beat me, he conquered me, he robbed me,' will not still their hatred.
>
> Those who do not entertain such thoughts as 'He abused me, he beat me, he conquered me, he robbed me,' will still their hatred.
>
> Not by hatred are hatreds ever pacified here (in the world). They are pacified by love. This is the eternal law.[42]

Reflection

Do you agree with these verses from *The Dhammapada*? How might you go about stilling unhelpful thoughts?

The rise of the Mahayana

Mahayana (literally 'great vehicle,' in the Indian language Sanskrit) originated in the Indian subcontinent from the first century BCE as a response to the rather narrow way in which the Buddha's teachings had come to be practised. The emphasis had become practising just for one's own Enlightenment. A new set of scriptures was written in Sanskrit, rather than the north Indian languages, including Pali, in which the early Buddhist discourses circulated. The Mahayana canon was transmitted to other countries such as China and Tibet, where the texts were translated into the local languages and a few new ones were written. The texts are called *sutras*.

In the Mahayana, the ideal practitioner is a bodhisattva who practises to gain Buddhahood for the sake of all beings. The bodhisattva has a very high aspiration, as shown in this vow, an aspiration it is impossible to achieve as an individual:

> May I deliver all beings from difficulties;
> May I eradicate all passions;
> May I master all dharmas;
> May I lead all beings to Buddhahood.[43]

Reflection

What is your response to this vow? Do you find it inspiring, or unrealistic and overwhelming?

Mahayana sutras expanded on what the Buddha said, and had a different emphasis. The Mahayana school valued both compassion and the bodhisattva ideal, and also wisdom in the sense of *sunyata*, that is, emptiness or openness. Ultimately, compassion and wisdom are inseparable. Let's look at a small extract from *The Heart Sutra*, which first appeared in China in the third century CE and has been valued ever since:

> Form is no other than emptiness,
> Emptiness no other than form.[44]

As you may realize, the text is somewhat mysterious, and I have felt ever since I first met it that it is speaking a deep truth, even though I don't fully understand it. 'Form' refers to the experience we have of what we take to be physical matter. One interpretation is that nothing has an independent existence. Such an interpretation seems to echo the experience of everything affecting everything else, as I experienced with the sea and beach.

Many Mahayana sutras are mythical, with the Buddha sitting in splendour among thousands of followers. His teachings may be through stories or images rather than the direct instructions of the Pali Canon. These teachings can speak to our hearts through the use of beautiful images and poetry. The following example has a mythical wise layman, Vimalakirti, giving advice to some women about becoming a bodhisattva.

> Sisters, there is a door of the Dharma called 'The Inexhaustible Lamp.' Practise it. What is it? Sisters, a single lamp may light hundreds of thousands of lamps without itself being diminished. Likewise, sisters, a single bodhisattva may establish many hundreds of thousands of living beings in Enlightenment without their mindfulness being diminished. In fact, not only does it not diminish, it grows stronger. Likewise, the more you teach and demonstrate virtuous qualities to others, the more you grow with respect to these virtuous qualities. This is the door of the Dharma called 'The Inexhaustible Lamp.'[45]

Many Mahayana sutras challenge the way we rely on concepts, since concepts can never capture reality in its full richness. For example, however many words you use, you can never capture your current experience in its entirety.

Reflection

What is your response to these Mahayana teachings?

In the space of a few centuries, the Mahayana flourished and spread in the east from India to South-East Asia, and towards the north to Central Asia, China, Korea, and finally to Japan in the sixth century CE. The following map shows the different waves of Buddhism: early Buddhism and Theravada we have already met, Mahayana we are looking at now, and Vajrayana we shall come to later.[46]

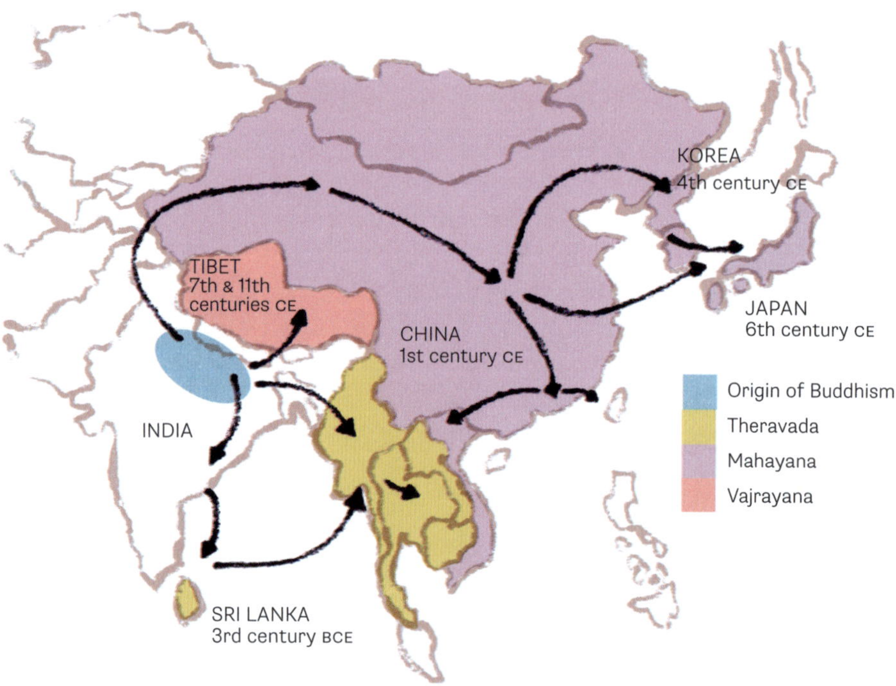

Madhyamaka

The Mahayana was a broad group of Buddhist philosophies and practices. Madhyamaka is one of the main schools within it. Madhyamaka was founded by Nagarjuna in the second century CE. It asserts that all phenomena are empty of 'self-nature' or 'essence', and that they have no intrinsic, independent reality apart from the causes and conditions from which they arise. The teachings are subtle and deep, so don't worry if the following example of a teaching of Nagarjuna is difficult to understand:

> When emptiness is possible,
> Everything is possible;
> Were emptiness impossible,
> Nothing would be possible.
>
> In projecting your faults onto me,
> You forget the horse you are riding.[47]

Yogacara

Yogacara (Sanskrit: 'yoga practice'; 'yoga' in this context means 'meditation') is an influential school of philosophy and psychology that developed in Indian Mahayana Buddhism sometime in the fourth to fifth centuries CE. It is also commonly known as Consciousness-Only (*Cittamatra*).

The key idea behind the Yogacara is that there is just experience right now, and that is all there is. We tend to think that experience belongs to somebody who is behind the experience and who is experiencing it, and that there is a world out there that is being experienced and exists independently. So we believe that there is an independent subject and an independent object. According to the Yogacara this is a mistake.

Consequences of the Yogacara point of view are, firstly, that ideas are experiences, so they are just ideas rather than realities beyond the experiencing situation. Secondly, memories are not windows into the past, but experiences in the present.

> The various things that are described conventionally as 'self' and 'object' in fact all arise within the elaboration of consciousness.[48]

Zen

Zen is the Japanese name of a Mahayana Buddhist school practised originally in China as Ch'an, and subsequently in Korea, Japan, and Vietnam. Zen emphasizes the role of sitting meditation (zazen) in pursuing Enlightenment.

A central part of all Zen sects is the notion of 'Dharma transmission,' the claim of a line of authority that goes back to the Buddha. Originally this derived from the description of Zen attributed to Bodhidharma, who lived in the fifth or sixth century and is credited with bringing Buddhism from India to China:

> A special transmission outside the scriptures;
> Not depending on words and letters;
> Direct pointing to the mind:
> Seeing into one's true nature and attaining
> Buddhahood.[49]

Some Zen schools use brief sayings, called koans. Koans often appear as paradoxical or linguistically meaningless dialogues or questions. The 'answer' to the koan involves a transformation of perspective or consciousness, which may be either radical or subtle. Koans are a tool to allow the student to approach Enlightenment by essentially 'short-circuiting' the logical way we order the world. The most well-known example of a Zen koan is: 'Two hands clap and there is a sound. What is the sound of one hand?'

There is also a tradition of using poetry and art to express practice.

> A cold night – sitting alone in my empty room
> Filled only with incense smoke.
> Outside a bamboo grove of a hundred trees;
> On the bed, several volumes of poetry.
> The moon shines through the top of the window,
> And the entire neighbourhood is still except for the cry
>   of insects.
> Looking at this scene, limitless emotion,
> But not one word.[50]

Pure Land

Pure Land Buddhism, also known as Amidism, is currently one of the dominant schools of Buddhism in East Asia. It is the devotional or 'faith'-oriented school of Buddhism, emphasizing chanting, and has become a mainstream branch of Mahayana Buddhism.

The main idea behind Pure Land Buddhism is that Enlightenment is difficult to obtain without the assistance of the Buddha. Instead of solitary meditative work towards Enlightenment, Pure Land Buddhism teaches that devotion to Amitabha, also called Amitayus, a Buddha figure that is particularly compassionate, will lead followers to the pure land (reminiscent of heaven), from which Enlightenment will be easier to attain.

In this extract from a Pure Land sutra, the Buddha is speaking to Sariputra, one of his chief disciples. 'Tathagata' is another name for the Buddha, and 'arhat' means someone who is enlightened.

> To the west, Sariputra, there is a buddha-field, a world system, named Sukhavati which lies beyond countless hundreds of thousands of other buddha-fields. At the present time, a tathagata, an arhat, a perfectly awakened buddha named Amitayus dwells there, teaching the Dharma. Why do you think, Sariputra, that world system is called 'Sukhavati,' the 'Realm of Happiness'? In that world system, Sariputra, in Sukhavati, living beings experience no physical or mental suffering, and there are endless causes of happiness.[51]

The sutra goes on to describe the pure land Sukhavati and the beings who live there. Such a sutra needs to be read many times and simply absorbed, ideally in a meditative state of mind.

Reflection

Do your best to imagine what Sukhavati would be like, both the sights and the sounds.

Vajrayana

The Vajrayana is an extension of Mahayana Buddhism. Rather than consisting of philosophical differences, it adopts additional techniques.

Vajrayana exists today in the form of two major sub-schools:

- Tibetan Buddhism, found in Tibet, Bhutan, northern India, Nepal, south-western China, Mongolia, and parts of Russia;
- Shingon Buddhism, found in Japan.

The key advantage Vajrayana Buddhism claims to provide is an accelerated path to Enlightenment. This is achieved through use of tantra techniques, which are practical aids to spiritual development, and esoteric transmission. Whereas earlier schools might provide ways to achieve nirvana over the course of many lifetimes, Vajrayana techniques claim to make full Enlightenment or Buddhahood possible in a much shorter timeframe, perhaps in a single lifetime. Vajrayana Buddhists do not claim that Theravada or Mahayana practices are in any way invalid, only that they represent slower paths.

The most important aspect of the tantric method is to 'use the result as the path,' which means that, rather than placing full Enlightenment as a goal far away in the future, one tries to identify with the enlightened body, speech, and mind of a Buddha. In order to achieve this self-identification with a Buddha-form, much symbolism and visualization is used in Buddhist tantric techniques.

Tantric techniques include:

- repetition of special ritual phrases (mantras),
- use of various yoga practices, including breath control and special hand positions (mudras),
- use of ritual objects such as the vajra and bell, hand drum, and many other symbolic tools and musical instruments.

Tantric Buddhism also places great importance on the guru-disciple relationship, for example through ritual 'empowerments' or 'initiations' wherein the student obtains permission to practise in a particular way, such as taking up a special visualization.

One archetypal figure who is particularly important in Tibet is Avalokitesvara. There is a story that, long ago, Avalokitesvara made a vow to save all living beings in Tibet, and that, if he should ever think of his own happiness, then his head would crack into ten pieces and his body into a thousand pieces. He made an enormous effort to help these beings, but then realized that not even one hundredth had been helped. He was seized by a bitter sorrow, and thought that his efforts were no use and it would be better to be happy himself.

At that moment, his head split into ten pieces and his body into a thousand pieces. Avalokitesvara cried out in pain, and Amitabha Buddha (the same figure we met in Pure Land Buddhism who personifies the compassionate aspect of the Buddha) appeared and put Avalokitesvara together again with ten heads plus his own head on top, and a thousand arms, with an eye in each hand. Then Avalokitesvara was better able to help people.

> How sweetly mysterious is the transcendental sound of Avalokitesvara. It is the 'primordial sound of the universe' [...]. It is the subdued murmur of the sea-tide setting inward. Its mysterious sound brings liberation and peace to all sentient beings, who in their distress are calling for aid; it brings a sense of permanency to those who are truly seeking the attainment of Nirvana's peace.[52]

Reflection

What conditions best help us to respond to the suffering of others without becoming overwhelmed?

Modern Buddhism

In the twentieth century, Buddhism started to make an impact outside Asia. This started with colonialism, and continued when travellers from Europe and later America began to explore Asia, and when people, including Dharma teachers, migrated away from Asia. As it has become popular in new cultures, Buddhism has adapted to the cultures it has found itself in, for example, by becoming more secular or more psychological or more individualistic.

Some of these adaptations reflect the tendencies of the people who are starting to practise Buddhism. So for example, in the UK, people can tend to be self-critical. Counteracting that tendency can be a useful practice, as many people find wishing themselves well both challenging and helpful. There are also tendencies to underestimate the importance of connections with others, to ignore any mythical references, and to practise just for self-improvement. So Buddhism can easily be watered down into simply individual well-being. It can still be helpful, but it can lack the radical element that brings a complete end to suffering.

Those of us practising in countries without a long-standing Buddhist tradition are pioneers. We are experimenting with ways of practising that are effective in our culture. The movement that I am part of is called the Triratna Buddhist Order and Community. Triratna is one of many modern schools, and is still developing. Its name means 'three jewels', as the three jewels of Buddha, Dharma, and Sangha are central to our practice. Over the years it has become clearer to me that a commitment to the three jewels means:

- regarding the Buddha as a spiritual ideal,

- meditating regularly,
- developing ethical sensitivity,
- practising together,
- discussing the Dharma with each other.

Let me tell you something about the history of my involvement to give a sense of what practising in this way and participating in sangha can be like. Everyone's experience will be different, but there are likely to be some common features and lessons for everyone. I'm providing some reflections to help bring these out.

In 1996, I was working at Cambridge University Press, and it became clear that either a colleague or I would be promoted. I relished the prospect of the challenge of more responsibility, but also respected my colleague, and it made me reflect on what was important to me in life. I realized that most important to me was to live my life well and in such a way that it would make a positive difference to others. I had read some books about Buddhism, and a friend had been to the local Buddhist centre to learn to meditate and recommended it, so I decided to go along to meditation classes there. The centre was part of the Triratna Buddhist Community, then called the Friends of the Western Buddhist Order.

Reflection

What conditions do you think could motivate you to visit a local Buddhist group?

The man who led the meditation classes was very friendly and inspiring. Over the course of six weeks, he taught us two meditations: the mindfulness of breathing and a meditation that involved wishing ourselves and others well. He had a long name that was difficult to remember, and it gradually came out that the name was given to him when he was ordained, and that the Buddhist order he belonged to was neither lay nor monastic. He wore what was called a kesa around his neck when teaching, and I heard that this symbolized a robe. It had on it a picture of the three jewels, a gold jewel symbolizing the Buddha, a blue jewel for the Dharma, and a red jewel for the Sangha. The male Order members were called *Dharmacharis* and the female *Dharmacharinis*, which means those who 'live or walk in the Dharma.'

This teacher and most of the other Buddhists I met were working in a Buddhist gift business and living in communities. The Buddhist business gave them an opportunity to work alongside other Buddhists in a spirit of generosity and with a focus on ethics. Everyone was paid according to their needs rather than the work they did, and there were regular opportunities to discuss their practice, as there were in the communities. The communities were single-sex, and community members would meditate together in the mornings and share tasks. Those who worked in the Buddhist business and lived in a community talked about it being a very intense way to practise.

I was happily married and did a job I enjoyed and that felt very worthwhile, so the way of living I heard about wasn't attractive to me. Nonetheless, I gained a lot from the classes and other activities that were happening at the Buddhist centre. In the years since then, the main Buddhist business in Cambridge has folded and, although there are still some communities, nowadays many of the sangha live with partners or by themselves, and most work in a non-Buddhist context. So, although in the early days of my involvement I felt myself to be an oddity, that is no longer the case.

Reflection

What sort of lifestyle appeals to you? What do you think would be the advantages and disadvantages of living and working with other people who are practising, meditating, and committed to the Buddhist path?

I found meditation quite difficult, as my mind wandered all the time, but somehow it made a difference to me and I felt happier and more confident. We were invited to talk about our experience in the classes, and I tended to stay quiet as I feared that there were right and wrong answers. It took some time for me to realize that whatever I was experiencing was simply what was happening, and it was unhelpful to judge it.

After a second course about going deeper in meditation, we had a weekend retreat that lasted from Friday evening to Sunday lunchtime. It was the first of several very powerful weekends away. It amazed me how spacious those weekends seemed, and how much difference they made to my mind. I would come away glowing and feeling quite tender. They also provided a good context for coming to know others who were practising, and helped me to develop friendships.

Reflection

What aspects of going on retreats might appeal to you? Information about retreats is given in chapter 8.

There was a small team supporting the classes. Apart from the leader, the team members were mitras, a Sanskrit word that means 'friend'. These supporters had been practising for a while, and had been through a simple ceremony to become mitras. The requirements for becoming a mitra have changed since those days; nowadays, they are that you think of yourself as being a Buddhist, you are trying to follow the five precepts, and you want to practise in the context of the Triratna Buddhist Community, at least for the present. Mitras normally have access to a study course lasting several years, which gives a good grounding in the Dharma. There are also special retreats for mitras.

We were told that spiritual friendships were very important and could help with practice. I was impatient to have friends like that. Over the previous eighteen years, I had been working full-time and bringing up two children with my husband, while he had studied medicine and started on his first very demanding medical jobs. There had been very little time to spend with friends. Now that the children had left home, I had more time, but it was hard to know how to go about developing meaningful friendships. It was great to discover that there was a culture of asking to meet up with people in order to get to know them better, so I overcame my natural shyness and invited other sangha members to lunch.

I was fascinated by the way Order members would think. Often their comments on difficulties I was having were surprising; sometimes they felt very supportive and sometimes rather challenging. I learned a lot from them, and very much enjoyed the time I spent with them. One example was meeting an Order member who had just spent over a year on a solitary retreat, and talked about the value of doing nothing at a time when I was very busy both in my job and around the Buddhist centre. I could recognize that there was a value in what he said, even though it challenged my way of feeling of value in the world.

Reflection

Are you attracted to experiencing spiritual friendships? If so, what attracts you? How might you go about developing such friendships?

After the meditation courses, there was a different team teaching some basic Dharma. The teaching was very clear, and I felt as if I were a child in a sweet shop with lots of fascinating things to learn. I wanted to go deeper and be more involved, and took whatever opportunities there were.

The main reservation I had was about the gender balance and whether women were taken seriously. During my first year visiting the Buddhist centre, I only met male Order members. Where were the women? Also, the attitudes towards gender were not the supportive ones I was used to at my work and home. It made me question whether this was a suitable movement for me. However, after the first year, I did meet women Order members, and I was impressed by them as I came to know them better. What also influenced me in staying with this movement was that women and men had the same ordination. I decided that Triratna might not be perfect, but it was good enough to support me on my spiritual journey and I asked to become a mitra; a few months later, I also asked for ordination.

Reflection

What features are important to you about any Buddhist group you become involved with?

At the mitra ceremony, several people became mitras. It was a simple ritual, which included each mitra-to-be having someone who knew them rejoicing in them, that is, talking about their good qualities. We all said some verses taking refuge in the three jewels of Buddha, Dharma, and Sangha, and chanted the five precepts, the precepts we met in chapter 4. At the end, I was showered with cards and gifts in a way that had never happened before in my life. It was a very joyous occasion. Some of my family attended, and it was a good opportunity for them to understand better what Triratna was like.

Soon after becoming a mitra, I started attending a study group of new women mitras that was led by two Dharmacharinis (female Order members). We studied various topics, including the noble eightfold path, some Pali suttas, what it means to be a bodhisattva, some Mahayana sutras, and some Tibetan symbolism. So we were inspired by teachings from many different schools of Buddhism. Much of the material was based on lectures given by Sangharakshita, the founder of Triratna. The study group lasted for three years, and I particularly enjoyed doing projects, which involved exploring more deeply some aspect of Dharma that was relevant to the topic we were studying at the time. I eventually came to very much appreciate studying just with women, although it took some time for me to become comfortable with sharing my experience openly.

Reflection

It is natural and sensible to be cautious about how much you share with others. When do you think that it might be helpful? What helps you to be more open, and when do you find it hard?

During this time as a mitra, I started going on longer retreats of one or two weeks. Some of them were meditation retreats, which were held mostly in silence. For me, silence was a relief and relaxing, but other people could find it challenging. Some were study and practice retreats at Tiratanaloka, a retreat centre that holds retreats preparing women for ordination. These retreats involved reading some study material beforehand and then discussing it in small groups. We also meditated and did rituals together. The women leading these retreats were very impressive, especially in the way they talked about their own tendencies and how they practised with them. They showed me how I might practise myself.

I found it helpful to go to Tiratanaloka once or twice a year, as it helped me to take my practice deeper, and returning to the same place helped me see how I was changing. During these years as a mitra, I developed several friendships, mostly with women Order members and mitras, but also with a few men. I learned a lot from each of my friends, and appreciated how they supported and encouraged me. Each person had their own strengths, and I learned from their perspective. One aspect of Triratna I appreciated was having several teachers, and not just one as in many other Buddhist schools.

Reflection

Do you like the idea of having one teacher or many? Why or why not?

It's probably a good idea to pause here and say something about Sangharakshita, the founder of Triratna. He was an Englishman, born in 1925, who felt a pull towards Buddhism from his teenage years. During the Second World War he was trained as a signalman, and he was delighted to be sent to Asia, including time in India. At the end of the war, he stayed in India and travelled around, becoming ordained as a Buddhist monk. After a few years, he ended up in Kalimpong, on the border of India, Nepal, and Tibet. There he met and was taught by several Tibetan lamas (Buddhist teachers) who were escaping from the Chinese invasion in Tibet.

In the 1960s, Sangharakshita returned to England. He realized that there was a need for a Buddhist order so he started giving meditation classes and, in 1968, performed the first ordinations into what was to become the Triratna Buddhist Order. Since then, the Order has grown to comprise about 2,500 Order members over about thirty countries. Sangharakshita died in 2018. He had already handed over responsibility for running the movement to a group of senior Order members.

Soon after I became a mitra, I found out that Sangharakshita had had some sexual relationships with male followers. Many of these relationships had ended happily, but some of his partners hadn't welcomed his sexual interest or were unhappy with the way the sexual relationship had ended. I felt disturbed and saddened that this had happened, and I could see that many Order members did too. I discovered that Sangharakshita was by no means alone in this sort of behaviour among Buddhist leaders in the UK and USA. It was particularly challenging reading reports in the media that focused on criticisms, when the vast majority of my experience of the Triratna Order was of people who were kind and wise.

It was another example of disappointment at a lack of perfection. I have a tendency towards wanting to be perfect myself, and of course constantly failing. I came to realize that I had strong expectations of others too and wanted them to be perfect, and that this was unrealistic. Forgiveness towards myself was an important step, and helped me to be more understanding of others too. We are practising because we are imperfect. The danger of wanting perfection is that we can end up rejecting everything, as perfection is impossible to find. Sangharakshita wrote some verses that express how it is more important to find conditions that are good enough:

Lines written on receiving from a member of the Western Buddhist Order the gift of his record collection, accompanied by some verses

Though one's food is not perfect
  It is enough to maintain health and strength.
Though one's house is not perfect
  It is enough to shelter the body.
Though one's job is not perfect
  It is enough to make both ends meet.
Though one's wife is not perfect
  She is enough to keep the home going.
Though one's children are not perfect
  They are enough to continue the family name.
Though one's Morality is not perfect
  It is enough to make meditation possible.
Though one's Meditation is not perfect
  It is enough to support flashes of insight.

Though one's Insight is not perfect
It is enough to reveal the emptiness of
mundane existence.
Though one's Guru is not perfect
He is enough to show one the Right Path.
Though one's fellow disciples are not perfect
They are enough to give moral support.
Though one's Generosity is not perfect
It is enough to loosen the bonds of attachment.
Though one's Patience is not perfect
It is enough to put up with having to live in the city.
Though one's Vigour is not perfect
It is enough for daily practice.
Though one's Wisdom is not perfect
It is enough not to be fooled by worldly things.
Though one's record-collection is not perfect
It is enough to make an acceptable offering.
Though one's verses are not perfect
They are enough to show one's sincerity.
Though one's letters are not perfect
They are enough for keeping in touch.
Though one's appearances are not perfect
They are enough for friendly recognition.
Though this acknowledgement is not perfect
It is enough to show deep appreciation.[53]

Reflection

If you have a tendency towards perfectionism, in what ways do you think it would be helpful to be more relaxed, and what would be the dangers?

Although it is important not to be fixated on perfection, of course, it is also important to take steps to be vigilant and make an effort to ensure that people are not exploited. Many years ago, senior Order members in Triratna started to actively discourage teachers from having sexual relationships with people who came along to their classes, and more recently Triratna centres have brought in safeguarding policies to make ethical guidelines more explicit.

Eventually I was considered ready for ordination. This happens when the Order members who know you well feel that your practice is effective and has enough momentum to keep going as long as you are in reasonably favourable conditions. By chance, I was offered an ordination retreat in India, on which both Indian and Western women were ordained.

It was interesting to see an emphasis in India on devotional practice rather than study, and that work in the community was a significant part of the practice there. Buddhism had been almost non-existent in India for many centuries, but there had been a revival of interest when Dr Ambedkar converted to Buddhism in 1956, and encouraged his followers to do the same as an escape from the caste system. Sangharakshita had given talks to large numbers of people in India, particularly later in 1956, after Dr Ambedkar had died. Order members from the UK helped to establish the extensive Triratna community there is today in India. At the time of writing, more than a quarter of the Triratna Order lives in India.

Ordination confers no special status or specific responsibilities, but Order members do have three duties:

- keeping one's personal practice in good repair and deepening it;
- staying in harmony with other Order members;
- being a bridge to help others join if they want.

After ordination, practice can be taken to another level. Firstly, I joined a chapter. Chapters consist of a small group of Order members, where possible of the same gender. Chapters usually meet weekly, and members share their lives and experiences with practice, especially around ethics. I find my chapter very encouraging and supportive, and they also give honest feedback to help me live my life better.

Reflection

In what ways do you think that it might be helpful to meet with a small group of friends regularly? Of course, you can do this without being ordained.

Most months, I also go to monthly meetings of Order members. These vary from just a day with other Dharmacharinis in Cambridge to several days with Order members from around the world. Every year I go on retreats – some retreats just for Order members, some for a wider range of people, and some solitary.

The Order is very much a network of friendships, and these meetings and retreats help to keep the relationships alive. The symbol of the Order is the thousand-armed Avalokitesvara we met earlier in the chapter. Each Order member is like an arm. I find it comforting to know that I'm part of something bigger and that between us we can make a difference, rather than trying to have an impact on my own.

Recently, I read my journal from the time around when I first became a mitra, and I was struck by how upset I was so much of the time and how often I cried. Nowadays I'm much more filled with joy or contentment and rarely upset, at least about anything personal. Part of the change is through having retired and so experiencing less stress from work, but the change feels to be much more than that. It's interesting how the fruits of practice are gradual and can be hardly noticed, and yet build up into something relatively substantial over time.

Reflection

It requires a big commitment to join an order such as Triratna. What do you think needs to be in place for someone to be ready to join such an order?

To finish this chapter, I would like to mention a final distinctive characteristic of Triratna, which is the emphasis on the arts. Many Order members write or paint, enjoy music or simply enjoy beauty. I find that going to an art exhibition or to a concert can have a very positive effect on my mind, and I particularly enjoy poetry for the way it can touch the emotions and convey values and ideas in a subtle yet effective way.

Reflection

What do you see as the challenges of practising Buddhism in the society and culture that you are in? Are there any changes you could make in your life that would make it easier?

6 Exploring the Mystery

The topic of this chapter is one that some people find unappealing while others love it. We shall be exploring the less rational side of Buddhism, which involves symbols, images, stories, myth, poems, and ritual. This approach is helpful in many ways, and has already formed part of the narrative in this book. Let me give some examples from our everyday lives and previous chapters of this book.

- You are probably aware of **symbols**, such as a red rose for love, a dove for peace, and holly or a star for Christmas. In chapter 1, we met the three jewels as a symbol for the Buddha, the Dharma, and the Sangha. To picture them as jewels emphasizes their great value and how they can bring pleasure. In this chapter, we shall explore some symbols that are probably unfamiliar to you so the meaning will need to be explained, but you may also find that they speak to you directly. They can give some sense of the mystery of life.
- **Images** can aid communication. Let me give a practical example. First, sit up straight with your feet on the floor. Now try sitting like a mountain. Notice any difference. You may like to experiment with thinking of your mind as being like the ocean in meditation: there are lots of waves on the surface, but underneath it is calm.

One student who had been on a mindfulness and meditation course said that, before the course, his experience was like being caught in a tumble dryer; afterwards, it was like sitting outside and watching the tumble dryer going around. This is a vivid description of the difference such practices can make. We have met images such as an elephant's footprint and bamboo acrobats.

- In chapter 2, there were a lot of **stories** about the Buddha, and throughout the book there are anecdotes about my experience of practice. Stories tend to be memorable and enjoyable, so they are a powerful means of communication.
- Some of the stories are clearly **myths** – they are not literally true, but illustrate a deeper truth. One example is the Buddha touching the earth at the time of his Enlightenment and the earth goddess appearing. This myth illustrates the importance of the Buddha's many years of practice in helping him towards Enlightenment.
- There are **poems** in chapters 2 and 5. I have always loved the way poems can put across ideas so effectively, often in a way that touches the heart.
- **Ritual** is symbolic action. It forms part of our everyday lives in ways we are often barely aware of. Everyday examples are shaking hands, giving someone flowers, waving, even raising an eyebrow. In the final part of this chapter, we shall explore several different rituals, some of which are quite simple, and others that are more complex and done with others.

In this chapter, we shall first explore various traditional Buddhist images and then look at ritual. As much as you can, it is helpful to keep an open mind about how you might respond to this aspect of Buddhism. It might be helpful to reflect on your past experiences of ritual and what we might call 'religious experience'. Did you grow up with ritual? What are your views about it? Notice how they show up as you read this.

I've always enjoyed images and poems, and over time I've come to appreciate ritual as a way to express my gratitude to the Buddha. The rituals we hold when people become mitras and get ordained have always moved me deeply. I'm well aware that it can be hard to appreciate such rituals through reading a book though, as they need to be experienced.

Symbols and images

The shrine

Traditionally Buddhism uses a lot of symbols, images, and myth. Some of these symbols can be difficult for us to relate to as they are unfamiliar. They are worth exploring, however, as they can give a sense of the mystery in Buddhism in a way that it is hard to capture in words, and their beauty can help us to experience more positive emotions.

When we meditate communally in the Triratna Community, we like to have a shrine as a focus. We try to make the shrine beautiful in order to help our mental states become more positive. Then we usually have these objects on the shrine to remind us of our purpose:

- a statue, normally of the Buddha, to remind us of the direction we are moving towards and evoke the qualities of the Buddha's body and mind;
- some flowers that are beautiful and remind us that everything changes, as the flowers soon fade and die;
- candles that represent the light of understanding that comes with practice and reaches its fullness at Enlightenment;

- and incense that symbolizes the power of the ethical life, whose influence can spread and perfume its surroundings.

Reflection

How might you arrange a small part of your room to remind you of the qualities you are drawn to and what you find beautiful? It provides an opportunity to have a space that you can enjoy and is a reminder of what is important to you.

The lotus and the vajra

There are two common symbols that highlight possible approaches to the path. These are the lotus and the vajra. The lotus is a very beautiful flower that grows in water, a bit like a water lily, but both the flower and the leaves rise up above the water. It grows in mud, so it can symbolize how something beautiful can grow from our messy minds. Since it is a plant, the lotus naturally symbolizes growth and development, and a form of practice that is gentle and unforced. All the lotus needs to flower is supportive conditions, such as water, mud, and warmth from the sun. Similarly, we just need to put in place supportive conditions for our Buddhist practice, such as hearing the Dharma, having a space in which we meditate, and being in communication with others who are practising. If those conditions are in place, we can simply relax, and then we too can naturally flower. This is called a receptive way of practising.

A different approach is provided by the symbol of a vajra. The vajra is a symbolic development of a thunderbolt; it is indestructible like a diamond, and hence is often called a diamond thunderbolt. Nothing can make an impression on a

vajra, and a vajra can smash through anything that crosses its path. Transcendental reality has these irresistible, immutable properties, so the vajra is a symbol of reality and the wisdom that realizes it. It emphasizes the need for energy and determination in our practice. At the centre of the vajra is an egg shape, symbolizing unity, completeness, and perfection. One end of the vajra stands for the negative qualities that chain us to the mundane world and our bad habits, and the other end stands for the positive qualities that free us. The axis joining the two represents how even unskilful states can be used as a fuel towards Enlightenment. The vajra path involves experiencing yourself as you really and truly are.

Reflection

Which of these two approaches appeals to you more: the receptivity of the lotus or the energy of the vajra?

The wheel of life

There is a common image used in Buddhism to symbolize our mundane lives: the wheel of life. It originated in India and is often found in Tibetan temples; it illustrates how our lives often

seem to be going round and round on well-worn tracks. It also offers a mirror we can use to explore ourselves from different perspectives.

The first thing you may notice is that the wheel is held by a fearsome creature. He represents impermanence and how everything that we see here in this mirror changes. Although he looks fearsome, it is because of impermanence that we can change to become closer to the person we want to be. There is even the potential for a more radical change when we step off the wheel entirely.

At the centre of the wheel are three animals: a cock representing greed, a snake representing hatred, and a pig representing ignorance. These three poisons – greed, hatred, and ignorance – propel us into our bad habits, and make us travel round and round this wheel. Greed involves grasping after what is pleasant; hatred is how we push away what is unpleasant; and ignorance is how we ignore what is neither strongly pleasant nor strongly painful, and think that our responses of grasping and pushing away are helpful. The animals are biting each other's tails, which represents how the three poisons feed each other.

Reflection

Explore how your habits may be fuelled by these three poisons. For example, you may start gaming to enjoy a sense of achievement when you win, to avoid what is painful, and to ignore parts of your experience. These poisons influence all of us in many different ways.

In the ring around the animals, we see people rising up on one side and falling down on the other. This shows the choice we have between growing by acting ethically and falling back when we act unethically.

The ring further out shows pictures of six realms. Traditionally, these realms are the places where we can be reborn. I find it helpful to interpret them as psychological states that we inhabit according to our state of mind. In each world, there is a Buddha holding something that is helpful when we are in that realm.

- At the top, there is a heavenly realm, full of pleasure. It is the place we inhabit when everything is going well and we are feeling that everything is right with the world. The danger in this realm is that we can become complacent and think that we no longer need to practise. The Buddha in heaven is playing a lute. The lute reminds us that, just as music is always changing, so does everything else, and we shall leave this place eventually.

- Moving clockwise, we come to the realm of asuras or titans, a realm full of competitiveness, jealousy, and aggression. It is the realm that we inhabit when we are trying to do better than others. The Buddha here has a sword, which symbolizes wisdom. This symbolism is rather a challenge to understand. Perhaps the sword represents the fact that what the asuras need to do is to destroy the false view they have that winning will make them happy in the long term.

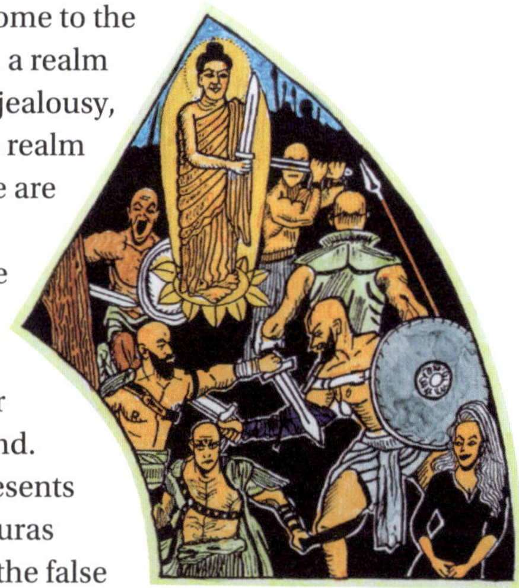

- Next comes the realm of animals. This is the realm of sensual indulgence, such as when we sit in front of the television munching snacks: the realm of couch potatoes, food lovers, and those obsessed with sex and pleasure. The Buddha here has a book, symbolizing the value of the arts and sciences to give meaning to our lives.

- At the bottom is the hell realm, a place of acute mental suffering. That suffering may take many different forms, both physical and mental. Fortunately, this realm too is impermanent, and beings leave it in time. The Buddha here offers nectar. This nectar has two possible results: one is ease and relaxation, and the other is Enlightenment. This second possibility may seem surprising, but sometimes suffering can be the spur we need to rethink our lives.

- The following realm contains hungry ghosts. These beings have large stomachs and small mouths, so that the food and drink they consume can never satisfy. It is a realm of desire that cannot be satisfied, a realm of longing for things and people. Often, when we get what we long for, it's not as satisfying as we expect. Oscar Wilde expresses it even more strongly in one of his plays: 'In this world there are only two tragedies. One is not getting what one wants, and the other is getting it. The last is much the worst, the last is a real tragedy!'[54] The Buddha here has food and drink that can satisfy. To take advantage of this nourishment, we need to discover what we really want deep down.

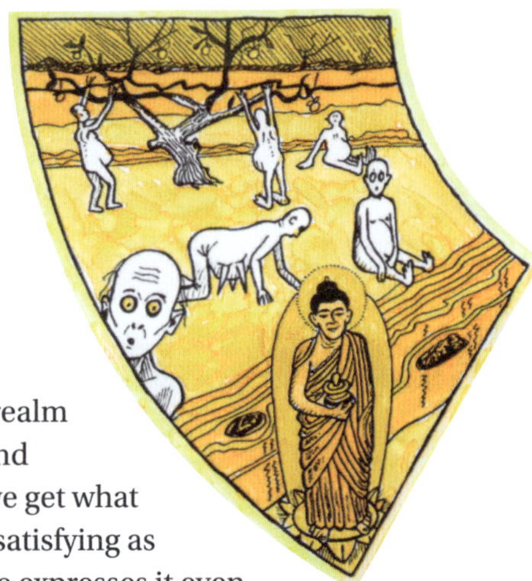

- Lastly, we have the human realm, in which there is both pleasure and pain. This is the ideal place to be in order to become enlightened, and the Buddha here holds a begging bowl and staff representing the pursuit of the spiritual life.

Reflection

Which of these realms do you recognize as being states you have experienced?

Further out again is a circle made up of twelve pictures. These pictures show how we pass from one state to the next. In particular, they show how our unhelpful habits of mind tend to lead to painful consequences. The most interesting part is how a trigger can spark a reaction, and how this keeps us on the wheel. Alternatively, if we can give a creative response rather than reacting, then there is instead an opportunity to step off the wheel onto a path that eventually leads to Enlightenment.

As an example, let's explore a way in which I can react. I can experience a trigger when I come into contact with something that someone has said or written that I regard as being untrue. The feeling that arises is painful, and the desire is to put them right as quickly as possible. The problem with this reaction is that I can pounce on what the other person has said or written, and that can lead to both of us becoming more entrenched in our positions, which can lead to hostility. Also, I can be wrong about what is true.

This sequence is illustrated by some of the pictures along the bottom of the rim. We shall start with the picture of a house with five windows and a door. This represents our five senses of sight, sound, taste, touch, and smell, together with the mind, which is regarded as a sixth sense in Buddhism. All of our experience comes from these **six senses**. In my example, I have used my ears or eyes.

The following picture shows a couple embracing. This represents **contact** between the six senses and an object. So my ears have heard someone saying something or my eyes have read something that I think is untrue.

Then comes a picture of someone with an arrow in their eye. This represents **feeling**, the experience of pain, pleasure, or neither that arises whenever our senses come into contact with an object. In my case, it is an unpleasant feeling from what I have heard or what I have read. This feeling happens naturally, and often we're hardly aware of this experience, and yet it provides a trigger for what happens next.

The next picture is shown as a man being offered a drink by a woman, representing **thirst** or craving. This is the point of reaction where we want what is pleasant, don't want what is painful, and ignore what is neutral. In my case, I want the painful feeling to go away.

What follows is **grasping**, which is shown as someone gathering fruit from a tree. This grasping involves trying to keep hold of whatever is pleasant, pushing away what is unpleasant, and ignoring what is neutral. I can try to make the painful feeling go away by telling the person that they are wrong. However, the other person can be upset by the way I try to correct them, and this can affect our relationship in a negative way. This affects what happens between us in the future. This is how we move round and round this wheel, powered by greed, hatred, and delusion in the centre.

So how can I step off this wheel into a more creative response? The important first step is that I recognize that the painful feeling is there in me. Then I can have a more creative response. The creative response may be simply to pause and become more aware of my experience in its totality, including how it feels in the body. It can also help to become more aware of the positive relationship I may have had with the other person in the past, and my desire for harmony with them. Just sitting, being present with my experience in a kindly way like this, can help me to calm down.

Alternatively, I may remember the importance of being ethical, of making sure any response is kind and helpful, and promotes harmony. So I may explore why they are saying what they are saying, and focus on finding our common values. In the process, I may also discover ways in which my views are mistaken.

These creative responses illustrate two possible ways in which we can start to step off the wheel: by giving wise attention to what is happening in the mind, or by focusing on being ethical. The path off the wheel is pictured as a rainbow spiral in the diagram on the next page, leading from the wheel just after the picture of a person with an arrow in their eye, and leading upwards to an image representing Enlightenment.

Reflection

Explore one way in which you can be triggered. What is the trigger? Is it pleasant or painful? In what way can you react? What might be a creative response?

The path to Enlightenment is shown here as a rainbow spiral. With a circle, we just go round and round and it is hard to get off, but going up a spiral suggests positive change. The spiral path is formed by a series of experiences that are increasingly refined and freer from unskilful states of mind. As each one grows and develops, it gives rise to the next. We have already come across this, and I'm quoting this passage again as it describes three possible first steps of being virtuous, non-regret, and joy on the spiral path:

> For a virtuous person, one whose behaviour is virtuous, no volition need be exerted: 'Let non-regret arise in me.' It is natural that non-regret arises in one who is virtuous, one whose behaviour is virtuous.
>
> For one without regret no volition need be exerted: 'Let joy arise in me.' It is natural that joy arises in one without regret.[55]

However, the steps aren't fixed or static. We keep returning to steps, each time, hopefully, at a higher level with increasing awareness and understanding. This is indicated by the shape of the spiral, which goes round and keeps rising.

The path is pictured as being rainbow-coloured. Rainbows are beautiful and ungraspable. They move as you move. Similarly, following the spiral path has a beauty and is not just a matter of following rules. Instead, it involves a sensitivity to the conditions we are in and the results of actions we take. Since we only see a rainbow when there is both rain and sun, it also symbolizes for me that all experiences are helpful on the path.

There are several different ways to describe the path to Enlightenment shown by the rainbow spiral. What is important is the first step onto the spiral path, as the steps after that come naturally once the first step has been done well. Unfortunately, it rarely happens that the first step only needs taking once, as we are built in a way that tends to delusion and self-clinging. Ignorance can guide us towards a small life, and tight and anxious mental states. But it's good to be aware that, each time we take a first step onto the spiral path, we are establishing a better habit, so are also progressing along the path.

Reflection

In what ways has your journey so far had the qualities of a rainbow spiral?

To progress along the path, we need to know the direction to go in, and that is what we shall explore next. We have explored the wheel of life, which is a symbol of the unenlightened mind. Now we shall explore a symbol for Enlightenment. This symbol is multifaceted, illustrating how there are many qualities to be developed as we move towards Enlightenment.

The mandala of the five Buddhas

An obvious symbol for Enlightenment is the Buddha. Over many centuries, as people meditated on the Buddha and his qualities, they found it helpful to have figures that personified different facets of the Buddha's qualities. In this mandala, each Buddha is of a certain colour and has certain qualities, which we shall explore. There are different ways of arranging the Buddhas, and we are going to look at them arranged in a special pattern as shown.

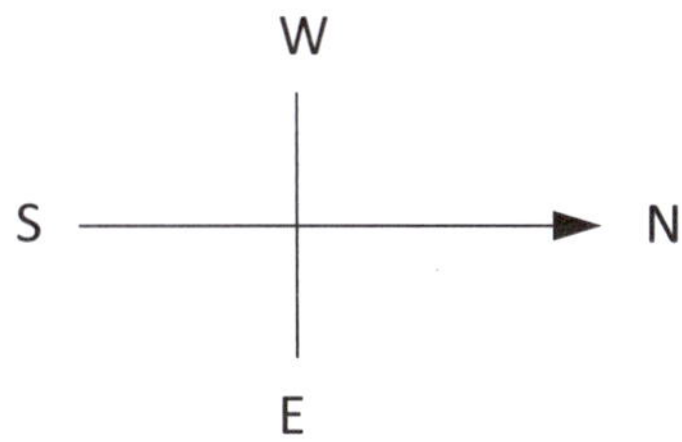

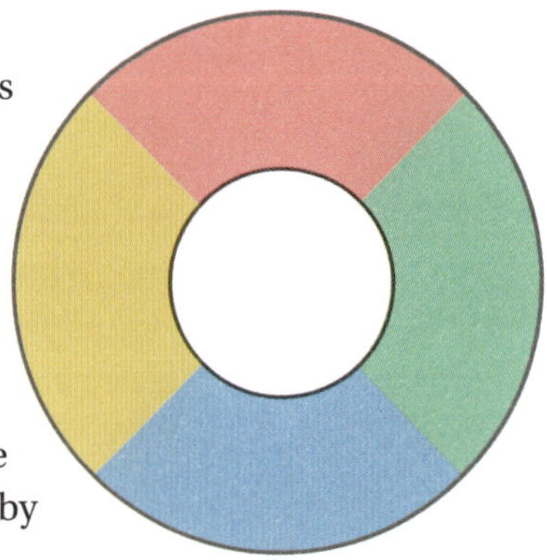

This arrangement has the form of a mandala. The word 'mandala' means 'circle', something round. Here the word means a harmonious arrangement of something highly valued. Often the mandala of the five Buddhas takes a simplified form, showing a floor plan of how the Buddhas are arranged rather like this, with each Buddha represented by his colour.

Let's explore each of the Buddhas in turn. There are a lot of associations for each one, and here I'm just going to give a flavour of the qualities of each Buddha. Traditionally, we enter the mandala in the east with the blue Buddha and travel around clockwise.

The first Buddha we come to is the blue Buddha called Aksobhya, which means 'immutable' or 'imperturbable'. His symbol is the vajra, and this gives a sense of how Aksobhya shows a lot of determination to keep practising. He has a mirror-like wisdom, which sees everything just as it is, just like a reflection on still water.

None of the reflections sticks onto a mirror, as a mirror doesn't react to what it sees. In the same way, Akshobya meets everything he observes with clarity and equanimity.

Next comes the yellow Buddha, Ratnasambhava, whose name means 'born from the jewel.' He has the wisdom of sameness, which cares for all people equally and sees their common humanity. His hand faces outwards in a gesture of generosity. He holds a wish-fulfilling jewel, which gives people whatever they want. He is associated with beauty and aesthetic appreciation.

The red Buddha in the west is Amitabha, 'infinite light.' His colour is red like the setting sun. He is the Buddha of warmth, love, and compassion, and symbolizes attraction and fascination. His symbol is the lotus, so he has the qualities of gentleness and receptivity. He has a discriminating wisdom that sees the uniqueness and value of everyone and everything, just as a lover sees what is special about their beloved.

We walk through a dark green forest at midnight to find the green Buddha, Amoghasiddhi, whose name means 'unobstructed success.' His symbol is a double vajra, a symbol of harmony, balance, and equilibrium, and also one that represents a lot of energy. He holds a hand up to represent fearlessness, and the double vajra reminds us that this fearlessness comes from developing all sides of ourselves. His wisdom is 'all-accomplishing,' and he achieves that by spontaneous, compassionate action.

We finish in the centre of the mandala with the white Buddha Vairocana, the 'illuminator'. His symbol is a golden dharmachakra, the wheel we met in chapter 3 as a symbol for the Dharma. It also symbolizes a great sun; as in our solar system, the sun is central and all life depends on it. In the same way, Vairocana is teaching and helping the Dharma to shine on all of us and transform us. His wisdom is the Dharmadhatu, the sphere of truth, which incorporates the wisdom of all the other Buddhas.

Reflection

Which is the Buddha that most touches your heart, that you most resonate with?

Before we move on, I would like to take a short diversion to talk about goals. I'm motivated to do so because I've just watched a TV programme about ice-skating, and a couple of the skaters commented that, if they didn't succeed in the competition they were taking part in, then all their hard work would have been in vain. This felt very sad.

When I'm talking about the five Buddhas being aspects of the goal of Enlightenment, the goal has a different purpose. Rather than the mandala being a place to reach and then you stop, the Buddhas are providing a direction to go in. Even if you never reach this goal, the changes you make will have a profound and positive effect on you and the people with whom you come into contact. Also, the Buddhas haven't stopped; their wisdoms involve being and doing in certain ways that never come to an end. My hope is that you will focus on enjoying this journey along the spiral path, while being illuminated by the light of the five Buddhas.

Reflection

What kind of goals do you find most helpful?

Ritual

Why ritual is valuable

Most of us rely on words and concepts to navigate the world. Words are certainly very helpful for communicating with others and for us to make sense of our experience. However, they have limitations. We can never capture a beautiful sunset or a stirring piece of music using words. Ritual, at its best, uses words, sounds, touch, smell, the movement of the body, and visual beauty to engage all parts of our experience and our mind in practice.

So ritual is a way of coming into wholeness, with body, speech, and mind all engaged and unified. It's a way of expressing what matters to us and what moves us. It's also a way of developing those parts of ourselves that are non-conceptual and allowing them to flourish. In the rest of this chapter, we shall be exploring some simple rituals that you may find helpful. Do feel free to experiment and find what is helpful for you.

Many of us feel rather cautious about ritual, perhaps as a result of our upbringing, or perhaps because of a feeling of discomfort with anything that feels overly religious. If you do feel suspicious about ritual, that is perfectly natural, but I invite you to read on. There are some simple rituals that are not particularly Buddhist and can benefit anyone. Also, your relationship with ritual can change over time.

We all have some experience of rituals. For example, there are rites of passage, such as marriages and funerals, or when someone leaves a place of work. Also, you are likely to be familiar with rituals that are symbolic actions, such as shaking hands or giving someone red roses. There is a shared understanding of what such actions mean, and they can express your intentions in a way that feels more meaningful than using words.

Ritual as a practice of gratitude

When people have learned how to meditate and do so regularly and practise ethics, then usually there are positive changes in their lives. This change can lead to feelings of gratitude. Even the Buddha wanted to express reverence to the truths he had discovered, because he valued them. One action to express this gratitude is to bow. I usually bow at the end of a meditation session to show gratitude to myself for making the effort and to the Buddha for showing the path. You may see people bow to a shrine, and that may express gratitude to the Buddha or respect for the potential we all have to become enlightened. Even if you feel this kind of gratitude, you may just want to make a bow in your mind, as it may feel too strange to do the outward action. That is fine.

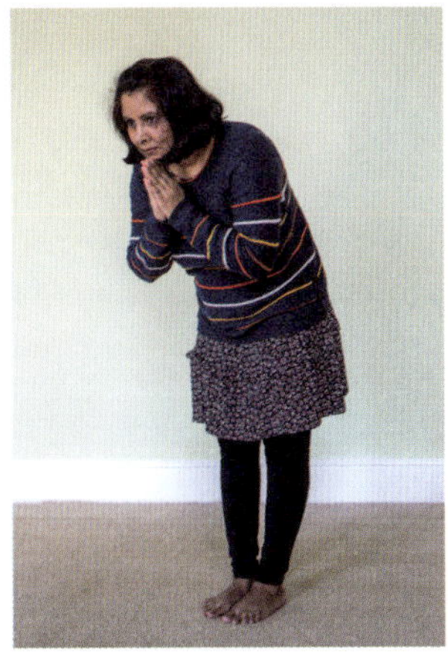

We can feel devotion towards the person who teaches us to meditate or teaches us the Dharma. This is natural too, and it is worth bearing in mind that, although it is good to feel gratitude to the teacher, it is the Dharma they are disclosing that is truly worthy of your reverence and devotion. Your teacher may not be perfect. They are rather like a mountain guide who has already been on part of the path and can show you where to put your feet, even if they have not reached the top of the mountain themselves.

Gratitude is a very positive emotion, which can help us to become more contented. We can cultivate it in relation to our ordinary lives, even if we don't feel it particularly for the Buddha or his teachings.

Practice

Near the end of the day, either write or say out loud three things that you are grateful for that day. If you want to make it seem more like a ritual, you could decorate the page on which you write, or ring a bell before and after speaking. It is good to do the practice regularly, perhaps once a week, or even every day. The things you are grateful for may be very ordinary. Try to vary what you write or say, so that it doesn't simply become habitual.

Today I am grateful for
a fun time with a friend
an enjoyable cup of tea
being able to walk

As an even stronger ritual of gratitude or reverence, in the Triratna Community we often make offerings to the shrine while a mantra is being chanted. These offerings may be incense, a candle, a flower, or something we have made ourselves. People make the offering in whatever way feels right for them, but they often go through these four steps:

1. Bow to the shrine.

2. Go onto knees, light incense or candle, and put the offering onto the shrine safely.

3. Move back slightly if necessary, and bow in a kneeling position one or three times.

4. Stand up and bow again then go back to their seat.

If you do decide to make an offering, it's good to remember that how exactly you go about it doesn't matter. In particular, if it is difficult for you to go down on your knees, it is fine to make an offering in any way that you are able.

Ritual and intentions

Ritual can also be used to help clarify and set an intention. An example of this is the dedication ceremony we use in Triratna. We say the dedication ceremony, usually in call and response, when we are starting to use a space for practice. Here is the first part of it.

> We dedicate this place to the Three Jewels:
> To the Buddha, the Ideal of Enlightenment to which we aspire;
> To the Dharma, the Path of the Teaching which we follow;
> To the Sangha, the spiritual fellowship with one another which we enjoy.
>
> Here may no idle word be spoken;
> Here may no unquiet thought disturb our minds.
>
> To the observance of the five precepts
> We dedicate this place;
> To the practice of meditation
> We dedicate this place;
> To the development of wisdom
> We dedicate this place;
> To the attainment of Enlightenment
> We dedicate this place.[56]

Practice

Write something similar that you can use to dedicate a room where you live or a time when you practise. Try saying it out loud and notice the effect.

Another example of using a ritual to support intentions is to write down something you want to keep doing, or something you want to avoid doing. If it is something you want to do, you can decorate the piece of paper and put it on your shrine, if you have one, or just in a special place, as a reminder. If it is something you want to avoid doing, you can burn it.

Practice

Do a ritual to support your intentions, either in the way suggested above, or in a way that feels right to you.

The value of beauty

Beauty can have a very positive effect on our minds. I often notice the effect when I spend time at an art exhibition, or when I'm in nature or a garden. Once when I visited the local botanic garden, with every flower, I stopped and savoured its beauty for the time it took to breathe two whole deep breaths. It was interesting how this slowed me down and how I felt more and more uplifted.

It's very easy to be grabbed by what is unpleasant, so it's useful to explore the effect of deliberately being more with what is pleasant. It may take some patience, as it's not what we usually do. It's lovely if you have a beautiful place to visit, but, if you don't, it can be interesting just to observe more closely what is ordinary, and it can sometimes come to seem more beautiful. I've found that I can appreciate the beauty in ivy and nettles, for example, when I take time to look at them carefully.

Practice

Find somewhere where there is some nature. It could be a garden or park, or just simply a tree in a street near you. Let your eyes rest on something that is relatively pleasant or interesting, take it in, and savour it for the duration of two whole breaths. Then move on to other objects. As best you can, simply do this without expecting anything particular to happen.

It is also possible to explore senses other than seeing. Buddhists in most traditions use chanting as a way to engage with beauty in sound. Here is a link to the Shakyamuni mantra as chanted on a Triratna retreat. Shakyamuni is the historical Buddha: Shakya was his clan name, and *muni* means 'wise man'. The mantra is a way of bringing the Buddha to mind: https://tinyurl.com/3tymy637.

Practice

Listen to the mantra as given in the link above or to another mantra, and either simply listen or join in if you want. Allow yourself to experience whatever you experience. This mantra lasts about ten minutes.

Puja

At its best, ritual helps us to find enjoyment in practice through engaging our senses in ways that are pleasant. Engaging our senses and emotions in a positive way is important if we are to maintain our practice, as the rational mind is not enough to keep us engaged. Ritual does this in various ways:

- having an image of the Buddha or an archetypal being that represents the qualities we value;

- using colour and beauty, particularly on the shrine, for example by using coloured cloths, flowers, and candles that we can enjoy;
- lighting incense, where the aroma illustrates how skilful actions spread and affect others;
- chanting, which can be uplifting, and making offerings to express gratitude and devotion;
- saying verses out loud connecting with our intentions or gratitude;
- using our bodies to bow and maybe prostrate, which encourages us to feel receptive;
- doing ritual with others so there is a sense of connection and common purpose.

It can also be inspiring and moving to witness the practice of other people in a ritual context.

You can only understand the power of a puja by attending one. It is hard to communicate it in a book. However, I'm going to share the final part of the most common puja we do in Triratna, because it consists of verses that are lovely to say after you have done something skilful. If you have reached this point in the book, then this applies to you.

The first verse talks about 'merit.' An alternative translation is 'goodness.' A person becomes full of goodness by performing good deeds. You acquire merit or goodness through kind actions, skilful speech, and a mind full of generosity, kindness, and wisdom. This verse is encouraging us to do these skilful deeds for the benefit of everyone, even creatures from outer space, rather than just for our own sake.

The transference of merit and self-surrender

May the merit gained
In my acting thus
Go to the alleviation of the suffering of all beings.
My personality throughout my existences,
My possessions,
And my merit in all three ways,
I give up without regard to myself
For the benefit of all beings.

Just as the earth and other elements
Are serviceable in many ways
To the infinite number of beings
Inhabiting limitless space;
So may I become
That which maintains all beings
Situated throughout space,
So long as all have not attained
To peace.[57]

7 Going Deeper

When the Buddha returned to the five ascetics after his Enlightenment, he first taught them about the need for a middle way between the idea that self-mortification can lead to Enlightenment and the idea that the ordinary life of sense-pleasures, such as having a house, job, and family, can lead to true happiness. He said that this middle way could be explored by means of the four noble truths and the noble eightfold path, and that this middle way would lead to transcending suffering. We explored these teachings in chapter 3.

The Buddha then went on to give a second discourse to the ascetics about how our experience works, explaining that some of the ways in which we regard some parts of our experience as being 'myself' or 'mine' are misleading. If we can have a more realistic view of our experience, we can have more equanimity and more freedom. As a result of this teaching, all five ascetics became enlightened themselves.

The way in which the Buddha divided up experience can be rather foreign to us, so we'll come to it a bit later. He described five aspects. We are likely to think of at least three aspects: bodily sensations, thoughts, and emotions. However, these aspects don't cover everything, and they overlap to some extent. But they can give us an idea of how we might divide up experience.

There is a story that illustrates the power of understanding how the Buddha divided up experience. One day, the Buddha's son Rahula came to the Buddha and asked for a teaching that would lead to full Enlightenment. The Buddha realized that Rahula did not have the maturity and wisdom to understand such a teaching, so he told Rahula that he should first teach others about the five aspects of experience that the Buddha had described. Rahula did that, and then needed to go through two more steps before he was ready for the teaching, but eventually he did attain Enlightenment.

One reason why it can be helpful to divide up our experience in this way is that it can help us to develop right view, the first limb of the noble eightfold path. It does that by helping us see more clearly what is happening in our minds. Our experience comes to us as a complex mass. If we can bring awareness to it and pick it apart, we can become more aware of our emotions and the stories we tell ourselves. Then we have more choice about what we do.

We need to do this with as much kindness as we can muster so that we don't shrink from what we find. So mindfulness and meditation are helpful to give us clarity, and right intention indicates the attitude we need.

It's a challenge to know precisely what the Buddha's five aspects of experience are. The Buddha chose aspects of our experience that made sense to the people he was talking to, but they can seem obscure to us nowadays. There are several different English translations used, and some of those translations can be difficult to understand. Also, different people sometimes have different understandings of what the Buddha said. I've done my best to find descriptions that are true to the Buddha and helpful. They will not necessarily be exactly the same as you will find everywhere else. I've been motivated by three principles:

- Firstly, as far as possible, the translations should be readily understandable and memorable. It should be reasonably straightforward to explore each aspect in practice.
- Secondly, the various aspects should show how our experience works, and help us to understand how dukkha arises and how we can be free from it.
- Thirdly, these aspects of experience are all processes that are constantly changing in response to each other, so, where possible, I've translated them as verbs rather than nouns.

In this chapter, I'll firstly describe each of the aspects and how they interact. Then we'll explore how each of these aspects can contribute to the misunderstandings we often have about ourselves. Throughout, we shall be noticing how the aspects all influence each other and are influenced by outside events, and how understanding this can be helpful in bringing equanimity.

Descriptions of the five aspects of experience

The five aspects of experience that we shall be exploring are described in what follows with my translations. They each require an explanation, as a single word cannot convey the full meaning. The Buddha gave an image for each aspect of experience,[58] and these too can be helpful in understanding their characteristics.

Rupa – form

'Form' is the most usual translation of *rupa*. 'Rupa' is a word it is particularly difficult to understand, as it is interpreted differently by different people. Rupa consists of qualities revealed to us by our senses (such as colour, sound, flavour, fragrance, and hardness) and whatever outside and within us gives rise to those qualities. So it includes that which we think of as physical objects. It also includes awareness of what is happening within the body, such as heat, cold, hunger, and thirst.

The Buddha described form as being like a great lump of foam carried along by the river Ganges. For us, a lump of foam is more likely to be seen when washing or washing up. You will have your own connotations with foam. Here are a few of mine. First, a ball of foam consists of many parts, and similarly our experience is multifaceted, with sense inputs from different parts of the body. A ball of foam may appear solid and unchanging, but the individual bubbles or sensations are fragile and impermanent. When sitting quietly, we can notice how bodily experiences simply come and go. Also, only the bubbles on the surface are visible – there are many bubbles inside the ball of foam as well. Similarly, we are only aware of some of the inputs from our body and senses, and we are unaware of others that are happening subconsciously. The lump of foam could also represent the way in which physical bodies are organized structures, seemingly solid, yet actually very delicate and impermanent.

Practice

Sit quietly and simply become aware of the experience of the body. Can you have a sense of the body as a whole? Are there any sensations of touch, such as what you are sitting on, that you only notice when you make a deliberate effort? Is there anything else that you notice?

Vedana – feeling

Feeling tone, or simply feeling, is the quality of pleasant, unpleasant, or neither pleasant nor unpleasant. It is a little more subtle than this brief description suggests, as there is a range of feeling, with some things being more pleasant than others. If you turn towards your experience right now, you can probably notice some element of all three – sensations you like, those you don't, and some that you don't really tend to notice normally.

Feeling is compared to a bubble that appears in autumn when it is raining and big raindrops are falling: a bubble arises in water and bursts when it reaches the surface. Again, our experience of bubbles rising through water may be limited, but we probably know that they are very fragile and will not last long, just like bubbles in the air. It is similar with our sense of pleasant and unpleasant. For example, our enjoyment of a particular food diminishes if we eat a lot of it at one time. Even the unpleasant experience of pain comes and goes in waves when we explore it. As a bubble arises in dependence on conditions, so does feeling arise in dependence on the other aspects of experience.

Samjna – recognizing

Recognizing includes our memories and thoughts about the past that enable us to label what we are experiencing. This includes concepts and views that we build up over time.

This recognizing usually happens so quickly we don't notice that we're doing it. However, it can become clear when we hear sounds, as we can't help but name what has given rise to the sounds rather than just being aware of pitch, volume, quality, and so on. You may like to experiment with looking around and noticing how much you identify and label rather than seeing splodges of colour. More importantly, we tend to apply labels to people and identify them as man/ woman/child. We can find it disconcerting when this is difficult. We can almost immediately label people as good-looking, sexy, smart, friendly, old, and in many other ways according to our prejudices. If we hardly know someone, it doesn't stop us.

All too often our labels are inaccurate, but we don't often realize it. For this reason, recognizing is compared to a shimmering mirage that appears at high noon in the last month of the hot season. A mirage gives the appearance of water although there is none. For us in temperate regions of the world, mirages mostly appear on roads when they are very hot. They are an example of an illusion that we can't help seeing even though we know that it's not real. Similarly, when we watch a film we can become engaged in what we see as if it were real, although what we see is actually light on a screen. In the same sort of way, many of our thoughts can be very compelling, even though we know that they may not be true. I experienced a strong example recently when I bought a tricycle to replace the bicycle I had ridden for many years. Despite being aware that the tricycle is so much more stable than a bike, I still feel fear that I'm about to tip off, because I cannot see the two wheels behind me. Rational thoughts are not enough to make me feel secure.

Illusions can easily arise when we think about other people. I find that it is very easy to make assumptions about what other people are thinking or feeling, particularly when I'm upset. It can be very compelling to try to make sense of what is happening with a simple story, rather than accept that there is some uncertainty. In particular, I've noticed how I can alternate between blaming others and blaming myself when there is some tension between us. The truth is usually much more subtle than either of those interpretations.

Practice

When your thoughts are troubling or are going round and round in your head, there are some things you can do:

- Simply observe the thoughts without feeling that you need to follow them. It may help to say to yourself, 'This is just a thought.'
- Notice any emotions that are also arising and that are giving birth to the thoughts. Is there sadness, anxiety, anger? It may help to name the emotion by saying, 'There is sadness present' or 'Here is anxiety.'
- Write your thoughts down. This gives an opportunity to see them more objectively, and may encourage you to take a wider and wiser perspective. You may also find it helpful to return to what you have written later and to notice if your interpretation has changed.

Samskara – deciding

This aspect is often translated as 'mental formations' or 'volitions.' It is the impulses, tendencies, and character traits that lead us to act in certain ways. It is the way in which we want to intervene or want to do something in response to our contact with the world. This aspect includes intending, planning, and reacting.

The decisions we make are based on many conditions: there are the conditions we are in at the moment and those that come from our past experience. For example, when I'm crossing the road, first I stop at the edge of the road and look both ways. This was something drilled into me as a child. If there is traffic coming shortly, I wait. If there is a car in the distance, then I use my experience from the past to judge whether there is enough time to cross before the car reaches me. If I'm in a hurry, I might take more of a risk. If the road is icy, I'll be more cautious. So there can be many conditions contributing to the decision to cross at a particular time.

The Buddha used the image of the trunk of a plantain tree to illustrate deciding. Plantain or banana trees have a trunk made of tightly wrapped leaves. The picture shows a cross-section.

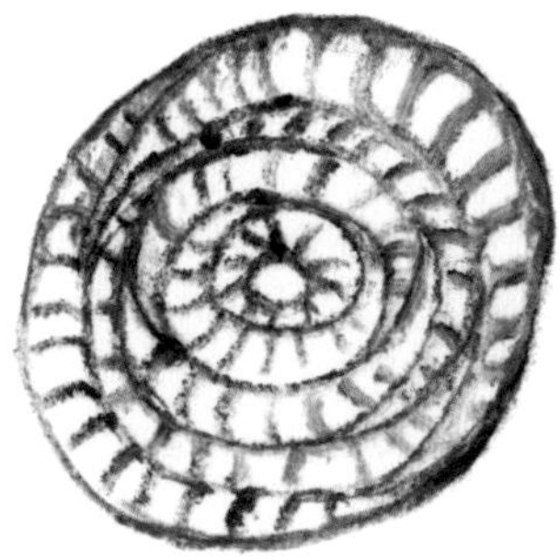

One way of understanding this image is that the leaves are the various conditions that contribute to deciding, and we see what seems to be a solid trunk, just as we assume that there is a solid self that makes the decision. Yet there is no solid core to who we are. We have habits that can seem solid, but they are the result of the conditions we have been in. The habits can be changed, albeit with difficulty.

One habit we have is to try to experience pleasure all the time and to avoid pain. However, the actions we take do not have the desired effect. There is no solid core to our experience of pleasure however we arrange our life, and no action we can take that ensures that we shall always avoid pain. The certainty that we long for is elusive.

Practice

Every time you buy something or take something you want, for example an item of food or drink, notice what has influenced you to have this desire and for how long you experience a pleasant feeling as a result.

Vijnana – knowing

Knowing is the awareness of all the above aspects. It is usually translated as 'consciousness'.

Our awareness can deceive us like a magic trick. A simple example you may be familiar with is how a sparkler can be used to draw a circle. We keep seeing the light from the sparkler even though it has moved on. Similarly, we think that we are the same person throughout the day, but in reality knowing or awareness is changing all the time in response to the play of form, feeling, recognizing, and deciding. An example of this that I experience sometimes is a reluctance to go out to an event because I feel that I don't have much energy. However, if I go, then I'm usually energized by the interactions with others and return home much happier.

As well as not noticing the changing nature of our experience, we are easily caught up in one of these aspects and unaware of the rest of experience. A powerful example that happened to me recently was being in pain following an operation. The pain dominated my experience, and I was unaware of other parts of my body that were not in pain; I had little interest in replying to emails or even eating. The Buddha compares knowing to the magical illusion made by a magician or a magician's apprentice at a crossroads. This is making the point that our interpretation of our experience cannot be relied upon to be true.

Practice

It can be surprisingly difficult to imagine feeling hot when you're feeling cold or to imagine feeling cold when you're feeling hot, to imagine feeling joyful when you're a bit depressed or to imagine feeling depressed when you're feeling joyful. So make a note of your emotions at regular times throughout a couple of days and notice what changes there are.

These five aspects of experience (form, feeling, recognizing, deciding, and knowing) are called *khandha*s in Pali and *skandha*s in Sanskrit. I shall use the Sanskrit term skandhas in future, as that is more commonly used. The literal translation is 'masses,' 'aggregates,' or 'constituents of experience.' You will find that the usual translation is 'aggregates,' but I find 'aspects of experience' more helpful.

Activity

To become more familiar with these aspects of experience, I invite you to put together a small collection of nuts and fruits, or other small items of food, and to eat them slowly one by one while exploring your experience. Take your time, and finish one item before starting the next.

At first you may like to simply notice what you can see and smell.

And then what you can hear and taste while you are eating.

Then you may like to become aware of the experience of pleasant and unpleasant, and how this influences which item you choose to eat next.

Lastly, notice how you recognize the different foods and how you are aware of all these processes as they happen.

It can be difficult to become aware of the different parts of your experience if you are unused to doing it, because the various aspects can appear to us as just a big blob of experience. If that is true for you, just do the best you can. It can take a little practice to pick apart the various aspects of what is happening. When you explore, you may well notice how different aspects influence each other. For example:

- seeing, smelling, and tasting enable you to recognize the foods;
- how pleasant you find a particular food influences whether you decide to select it again;
- when you finish eating one thing, or maybe before you finish it, you start looking for the next thing to eat;
- if you recognize a food from the past and remember enjoying it, you are more likely to choose it. If you disliked the taste in the past, you are more likely to avoid it.

As you explore further, you can find that each of the first four skandhas influences each of the rest. We can visualize this as shown here, where arrows show influence.

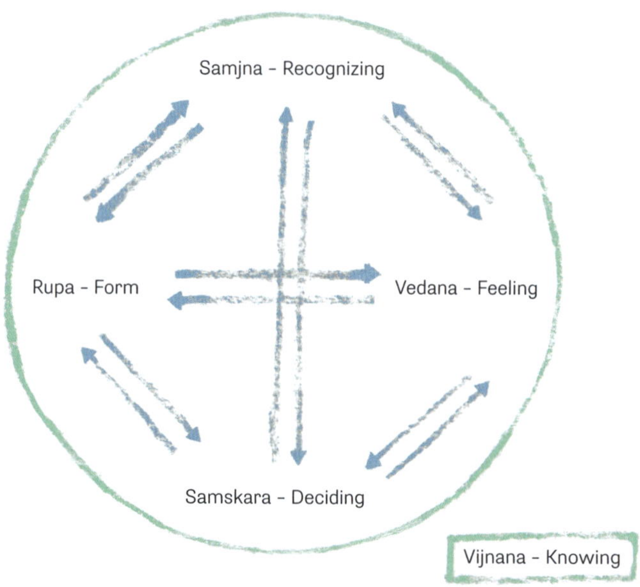

Some of the arrows are less obvious than others. I was very struck one time when I was on retreat that the way I labelled a sound made a difference to whether it was pleasant or unpleasant. If I thought that the sound came from a barn owl living above me then I thought it was pleasant, but if I thought that it came from children next door then it seemed unpleasant, so recognizing influenced feeling more than I thought possible.

Another surprise came when I went on a walk and tried to identify all the wild flowers. Once I had identified a flower, I noticed examples of it that I hadn't seen before. So recognizing influenced what I was seeing.

Yet another example is how I experience pleasure when I do something generous. So a generous intention can influence feeling.

Knowing is what enables us to be aware of the skandhas and how they influence each other.

Reflection

Find examples of as many of the arrows of influence as you can from your own experience.

How the skandhas can give us a sense of self

The five skandhas incorporate all that we might consider to be our experience. The images for the skandhas have illustrated their characteristics of constantly changing and being subject to conditions, and so being interconnected with each other and the world. Let's go through the five skandhas and explore more deeply how each of them is constantly changing and not separate from the conditions we are living in.

Form

Our bodies are constantly changing as we take in food and drink and breathe in and out. Our skin is slowly being shed and renewed from below. There are obvious changes that happen over time: first growing when we are children and then the effects of ageing. The changes are strongly influenced by the conditions we are living in. For example, being able to access healthy food helps to keep us well, and having enough sleep can help to keep us more alert. So the conditions we are in affect what we experience through the body.

Our experience of the world is complex, as it involves input from all the different senses. Each aspect comes and goes as we pay attention to it or not. Form provides the inputs which are then interpreted by the other aspects of our experience, often so quickly we hardly notice what is happening. We are often unaware of the subtle differences in what we experience. For example, our brains compensate for changes in light level and colour so that we experience continuity. I am very struck by Monet's twenty-eight paintings of Rouen Cathedral because he sees so many variations of colour, when he looks during different times and in different weather, whereas, when I look at buildings, I just tend to see the same building. Here are just three of the pictures to give a sense of the variety.

Practice

It can be liberating to realize that our experience keeps changing and we don't need to struggle to fix it. When it is raining, it is sensible to put up an umbrella if we have one. But, if we have no umbrella, we may have to experience becoming wet. If we can accept that this is our reality, then we shall suffer less and may come to discover that there is unexpected joy and freedom in the rain.

Do this practice when some element of your experience is a little difficult, for example, there is an unpleasant sound or smell, or the body is uncomfortable. Notice any contraction around that experience.

Then, as best you can, allow yourself to experience what is happening without trying to make it different. Simply let it be. You may find it helpful to breathe into what is difficult, and on the outbreath to soften and open.

We experience a cloud of sensations that depend on the conditions we are in. We can influence the conditions, for example by walking outside rather than sitting still indoors. In this way, we influence what we experience through the body and senses, but we cannot force our experience to be a certain way. It is the attempt to force our experience that causes us suffering.

Reflection

In what ways do you find it helpful to realize that the body and what we are sensing are always changing?

In what ways is it helpful to realize that our experience depends on the conditions we are in?

Feeling

There is a strong natural urge to cling on to pleasant feeling and push away unpleasant feeling. This can be a very powerful force in our behaviour. However, the project to experience only pleasant feeling is bound to fail. The capacity of any conditions to produce pleasant feeling reduces over time. However pleasant a cake is, eventually I don't want to eat any more as it no longer produces a pleasant feeling. By contrast, when I have been in an unpleasant situation for a while, then any relief from that situation feels pleasant. It is almost as if the amount of pleasant feeling and the amount of unpleasant feeling that I experience naturally balance out no matter what I do.

When I'm fully able to take this on board, then I realize that all I can do is act as skilfully as possible, as that is acting as much as possible in accordance with reality. Then I just need to accept whatever happens as a result and not fight it. It can help to be careful with language and, instead of saying to myself that I *want* a particular outcome, to say that I would *prefer* that outcome.

There is a lovely story that illustrates how mistaken we can be about what we want to happen. According to the story, there was once a farmer whose son managed to capture a wild horse. The neighbours said how lucky the farmer was, and the farmer said, 'Let's see.' The son tried to ride the horse and was thrown off and broke his leg. Now the neighbours said how unlucky the farmer was, and the farmer said, 'Let's see.' Then some men came to the village and took away the young men for the army. They left the farmer's son. How might the story continue?

Reflection

Notice what happens when something doesn't go the way you want it to. In particular, notice any unpleasant feeling and any stories that you tell yourself. As best you can, show yourself some compassion for any distress you feel by telling yourself that this is what it is like to be human. What would be a skilful way to act in this situation?

In order to experience pleasant feeling as much as possible, we can identify with our likes and dislikes, based on what we find pleasant or unpleasant. Yet these feelings are not as constant as we tend to think. For example, I find that I come to like people more as I come to know them better. The music I find pleasant can depend on my mood and how much I have heard it before, and similarly the food I enjoy changes according to time of day and what I have been eating recently. Just remembering this can help me to hold my likes and dislikes more lightly.

Reflection

Bring to mind any occasions when your likes or dislikes have changed. They may be very temporary, such as eating so much chocolate that you don't want any more. Or they may be longer lasting, such as learning to love a piece of music or no longer enjoying playing with toys you loved when a child.

Practice

It can be a continuing source of discomfort to dislike someone and find them unpleasant. See if you can change your attitude, either by focusing on their good qualities, or by getting to know them better. This is likely to be a challenging practice, so start with someone you find just mildly unpleasant.

Recognizing

Let's now explore recognizing and the associated memories, views, and stories we tell ourselves. It is interesting how we add interpretations, or recognizing, to our experience very rapidly. When hearing sounds, I notice how I label them as traffic or birdsong or a doorbell and so on. It is similar with what is seen or tasted or smelled.

Practice

Focus on sounds, and experiment with noticing the loudness, pitch, and quality of the sound without labelling. Notice any desire to label what is giving rise to the sound.

There are certain limitations to the way we think about things:

1. We usually use words, and words can never capture the complexity of real life. The simplifications that words bring about are useful in many ways. Life would be too complicated to think about constructively without them, but they also have their limitations. For example, it is easy to ignore the influence our mood has on the way we interpret things.
2. We find uncertainty unsettling. We want to make sense of the world, so we make an effort to come to a definite conclusion. Inevitably, this conclusion will sometimes be wrong.
3. Our views and the stories we tell ourselves are very influenced by what we hear and read. Some of us have a tendency to believe whatever someone else tells us, while others may have a tendency to be sceptical. Nearly all of our ideas come from others. Even when I feel that I'm being creative in my thinking, it's mostly that I'm putting together ideas from others that I've come across.
4. Everyone has their own values, and these values may lead them to act differently from us. They may want safety for themselves and those close to them, or they may think that fairness or justice or loyalty is important, or they may want to relieve suffering. So we may find it difficult to understand others if their values are different from ours.

These four considerations mean that we need to be careful about clinging on to our views and stories about what is happening. It is often a good idea to take a broader perspective if we can. This can involve trying to see the circumstances from someone else's point of view or bringing to mind how things change over time. For example, when we are blaming someone for something they did, it can be helpful to remember a time when they acted differently or to try to see what happened from their point of view. We can also remember when we acted in a way that was unethical, or that disappointed someone else, remembering our own motivation. The following practice can help us hold our ideas more lightly when we realize that our thoughts are unhelpful.

Practice

Sit quietly for ten minutes, and notice the thoughts that arise. With each one say, 'Thank you thought. Goodbye.' You can also do this practice with someone else where one person says possible thoughts one after the other and, with each thought, the other person says, 'Thank you thought. Goodbye.'

It is in the area of memories, views, and ideas that I can feel most connection with others, especially with the friends and family members with whom I share them. Sometimes I can feel quite strongly that I'm not entirely separate from these people I'm close to, or from others whose books I've read or whose talks I've listened to.

Of course, it is easy to cling to the stories I tell myself in order to make sense of the world. There are the stories about my life, which are as truthful as I can make them, but lack the subtlety of what actually happened. There are the stories about other people, which fail to take account of the way in which everyone changes according to mood and the conditions they are in, such as work or family situation, or the way people change as they grow older. It can be particularly challenging for me with grandchildren, as their interests and preferences change relatively quickly.

I've sometimes found it quite shocking how many of my thoughts are about me. It can feel like a relief when I'm so absorbed in something that I'm not thinking about myself at all. So there is probably a lesson there that it is a good idea to simply let go of many of my thoughts. This doesn't mean trying not to think about something, as that is impossible – it's more about just watching thoughts come and go like clouds in the sky. Some are big and dark, and some are small and fluffy, and they all pass and are insubstantial.

Reflection

Bring to mind a time you have made an assumption about someone that has turned out to be distorted. What idea about them had you had in mind?

Practice

Spend a few minutes simply watching your thoughts come and go like clouds in the sky.

One aspect of labelling is what we label as 'mine'. There can be *my* partner, *my* children, *my* house, *my* job, *my* religion, *my* dog, *my* cat, *my* clothes, *my* country, *my* likes or dislikes, and so on. To label in this way can give a sense of security, but this sense may not be as solid as we think: possessions may be sold, break, or be stolen; preferences may change; and people may act in ways we don't like. Many years ago, the man I married started a practice of avoiding saying 'my wife' when referring to me, and instead using my name, as he wanted to overcome any subtle idea he might have had of owning me. I took it up too, and we expanded the practice to include any use of 'my'. It had an effect of loosening our ties to things and expectations of people, both of which felt useful. It may well have contributed to us still being happily married after more than fifty years together.

Practice

Notice when you say 'my' or 'mine'. If you feel able, avoid using these words as much as you can. Notice any effect that has.

Deciding

Deciding includes intending, planning, and reacting. It involves actions of body, speech, and mind, so what we say and deliberate thoughts. We are deciding all the time, yet it strikes me that so many of our actions happen without much thought at all. We simply act on automatic pilot in response to what is happening around us. Although there are actions that we keep returning to and are habits, that doesn't mean that they are fixed. What we do depends crucially on the conditions we are in.

Practice

Go for a walk without any particular intention, and without any idea of where you want to go. Notice when decisions arise, for example when crossing a road, or needing to go either left or right. Notice how conditions unfold and how they give rise to where you go and what you do.

I find it fascinating how it is never enough to have an intention to do something. I can have an intention to lose some weight by avoiding eating cakes, but, if I go out for tea with a friend and they buy a delicious-looking cake and ask me to join them, it is very hard to resist. An overarching intention is just one condition among many affecting the actions I take. For that reason, I find it helpful not to have food in the house for snacking, so that it would take a substantial effort to indulge and I'm less likely to do it. It is easier to set up conditions that support healthy eating than to try to impose my will all the time.

Meditation practice is important to me. So I have put several conditions in place to support my meditation practice: an attractive quiet space dedicated to it, communication with those around me that it is important to me, a daily routine that includes meditation, going on meditation retreats to keep my practice fresh, and using recorded led meditations when input would be helpful. There may be occasional lapses when I'm ill or grandchildren come to stay, but these are rare because the conditions provide support.

Reflection

If there is something you would like to do in your life, what conditions could you set up to facilitate it?

Knowing

This aspect of experience involves knowing what is happening in the mind, and particularly the way in which the skandhas work together. We have seen how each of the skandhas is a flow. They influence each other like a dance, with input coming from form. Our experience is never fixed, even for a few seconds. It is constantly influenced by external conditions, and our experience of external conditions is influenced by the play of the skandhas. When we fully take this on board, we don't see ourselves as separate from the rest of the world. In particular, what happens to other people affects us, even if the chains of influence are hard to appreciate. What we do affects the rest of the world, much more than we tend to appreciate.

I have noticed that a lot of the distress that I experience comes from taking things personally. It can take the form of not feeling appreciated enough for things I have done, feeling blamed in ways that seem excessive, or thinking that I have sole responsibility for what is happening. It can be helpful to bring to mind that I and other people are just doing the best we can in the circumstances we are in. When I manage to do that, the dropping of resentment or sole responsibility can feel like a big relief.

Practice

Bring to mind a time when you felt unappreciated or blamed. Explore any sadness or anger with a soft and gentle heart. Try to understand the other person by bringing to mind any conditions that may have led to them acting in that way. This can be a challenging practice, so simply be appreciative of any softening that arises.

There are two main lessons we can take away from this chapter.

1. We are changing much more than we realize. One of the most common misunderstandings is to think that we shall feel and think in the future the same as we do today. When we truly understand that, we can relax much more about trying to make the future be a particular way.
2. The second misunderstanding is underestimating the influence of the conditions we are in on our experience and actions. It can be helpful simply to list the conditions that are contributing to our current experience, and thus take a broader perspective. In this way we can come to see the limitations of the stories we tell ourselves.

The knowledge that everything we experience is ever-changing and influenced by conditions can be very freeing. It can involve seeing our experience as a dance of conditions that words cannot describe. The nearest I have found to a description is in the following poem by Kathleen Raine, so I'm using it to finish this chapter and the main part of the book:

The moment

To write down all I contain at this moment
I would pour the desert through an hour-glass,
The sea through a water-clock,
Grain by grain and drop by drop
Let in the trackless, measureless, mutable seas and sands.

For earth's days and nights are breaking over me,
The tides and sands are running through me,
And I have only two hands and a heart to hold the desert
and the sea.

What can I contain of it? It escapes and eludes me,
The tides wash me away,
The desert shifts under my feet.[59]

8 Next Steps

Congratulations on reaching this far. This chapter gives some guidance about what it would be helpful to do next. It includes information on how to learn to meditate, books to read, talks and podcasts to listen to, and online resources to explore.

Learning to meditate and going on retreat

It can be so helpful to meet other people who are interested in Buddhism. However, opportunities to do this might depend on where you live. Any list of places where you can do this is likely to go out of date very quickly, so you will need to investigate what is currently available. You could look at https://thebuddhistcentre.com/text/triratna-around-world, which is a listing of all Triratna centres. Or you could google Buddhist groups near you; there is likely to be something nearby.

If you have not done so already, you are likely to find it very helpful to learn to meditate. Ideally, find some classes near you. A course can be useful to help you develop a regular meditation practice. Alternatively, you may be able to find a retreat aimed at newcomers. In the UK, at present, there are weekend retreats that teach meditation at Rivendell, Taraloka (women only), and Dhanakosa retreat centres, and possibly local Buddhist centres. Also Gaia House in Devon, UK, holds a variety of meditation retreats. In the USA, there are currently days teaching meditation at Aryaloka Retreat Center (Newmarket, NH).

Retreats can be life-changing. When I was starting, I found that weekends could be amazing in their effectiveness in a relatively short time. There was a sense of timelessness on retreat, and I usually emerged uplifted and feeling connected to the others on retreat. Even a day of practice could show the potential for positive change. You can find information about Triratna retreat centres and the retreats they offer, not just on meditation, at https://goingonretreat.com.

If you are unable to attend in person, there are plenty of resources and support for learning meditation at wildmind.org. There are many courses ranging from introductions to meditation to ones suitable for experienced practitioners, all with led meditations. The website also has interesting articles relevant to Buddhist practice. There are lots of good meditation apps too – Headspace and Insight Timer, for example, are two well-known ones.

Further reading

There are very many books that expand on the themes explored here. Listed below are ones I think you will find interesting. They are listed by chapter so that you can explore further the ideas in each chapter. At the end are some titles that don't fit into that framework and instead explore a particular topic, and also magazines that can be helpful.

Chapter 1

- Vajragupta, *Buddhism: Tools for Living Your Life*[60]

This book aims to convey a feeling for what a 'Buddhist life' might be like. It includes plenty of 'tools' – suggestions for how to live such a life.

- Danapriya, *It's Not Out There*[61]

Most of us constantly look outside ourselves for something: happiness, love, contentment. But this something is not out there. 'It' is within us. This book helps you to find it.

Chapter 2

- Vishvapani, *Gautama Buddha: The Life and Teachings of the Awakened One*[62]

This is a compelling biography of the Buddha. It is based on ancient sources and modern scholarship, and is written in an engaging way so that we are imaginatively taken to the Buddha's time in India.

Chapter 3

- Dhivan Thomas Jones, *This Being, That Becomes: The Buddha's Teaching on Conditionality*[63]

This book explores conditionality and its consequences, such as the spiral path, karma, the middle way, and emptiness.

- Paramananda, *Change Your Mind: A Practical Guide to Buddhist Meditation*[64]

This is a best-selling, accessible, and thorough guide to meditation.

Chapter 4

- Subhadramati, *Not About Being Good: A Practical Guide to Buddhist Ethics*[65]

A clear exposition of the principles of ethics and practical methods to embody them. It is written with passion, humour, delicacy, and sympathy.

Chapter 5

- Nagabodhi, *Sangharakshita: The Boy, the Monk, the Man*[66]

A biography of Sangharakshita, the founder of the Triratna Buddhist Community, written by someone who knew him well.

Chapter 6

- Vessantara, *Meeting the Buddhas*[67]

An engaging description of the main Buddhas and bodhisattvas.

Other books

- Prajnaketu, *Cyberloka: A Buddhist Guide to Digital Life*[68]

A witty and thoughtful account of how Buddhists can engage fruitfully in the online realm that forms a significant part of many of our lives.

- Vaddhaka Linn, *The Buddha on Wall Street: What's Wrong with Capitalism and What We Can Do About It*[69]

An insightful and engaging exploration of a Buddhist approach to economics.

- David Loy, *Money, Sex, War, Karma: Notes for a Buddhist Revolution*[70]

A fascinating look at how Buddhist principles can be applied to society.

- Shantigarbha, *The Burning House: A Buddhist Response to the Climate and Ecological Emergency*[71]

Particularly useful as a guide to how to practise with the difficult emotions that can arise when you're confronted with the climate and ecological emergency.

- Shantigarbha, *I'll Meet You There: A Practical Guide to Empathy, Mindfulness and Communication*[72]

This book explores empathy for ourselves and others, and can help you deepen your relationships.

Wisdom Publications publish many Buddhist books, including translations of the Pali Canon. They also provide courses, podcasts, and videos. Shambhala Publications too publish many Buddhist books including a few for children. They too have some courses and videos. It is also worth looking at the many books by the Dalai Lama, which are published by a variety of publishers.

Tricycle is a quarterly magazine, based in the US, that publishes a variety of articles from many branches of Buddhism. The Tricycle Foundation also provide some courses, e-books, and films for subscribers. *Buddhadharma: The Practitioner's Quarterly* is another magazine, this time based in Canada, which is not tied to a particular school.

Talks, podcasts, and the internet

Free Buddhist Audio (https://www.freebuddhistaudio.com) provides a wide variety of talks and podcasts from the Triratna Community. It includes led meditations, and you can search for topics that interest you.

Dharma Seed (https://dharmaseed.org) provides a wide variety of talks based on Western Buddhist Vipassana teachings. Many of the talks have been given on retreats.

Windhorse Publications has a podcast (https://www.windhorsepublications.com/podcast/) where authors, teachers, and experienced practitioners talk about books.

The Buddhist Centre (https://thebuddhistcentre.com) is part of the Triratna Community and has a lot of information about this movement. Sign up to the Dharma Toolkit (https://thebuddhistcentre.com/stories/toolkit/) to receive the latest information about resources and events, most of which are online.

Notes and References

1 *Culahatthipadopama Sutta* from the *Majjhima Nikaya*, in *The Middle Length Discourses of the Buddha*, trans. Bhikkhu Nanamoli and Bhikkhu Bodhi, Wisdom Publications, Boston 1995, p. 274 (pronouns have been adjusted to be gender-inclusive).
2 *Culamalunkya Sutta* from the *Majjhima Nikaya*, in *The Middle Length Discourses of the Buddha*, pp. 533–6.
3 *Tittha Sutta* from the *Udana*, in *The Udana and the Itivuttaka*, trans. John D. Ireland, Buddhist Publication Society, Kandy 1997, pp. 86–8.
4 *Culahatthipadopama Sutta*, pp. 269–77.
5 Analayo, *Perspectives on Satipatthana*, Windhorse Publications, Cambridge 2013, pp. 244–5 (slightly modified).
6 *Attadanda Sutta* from the *Sutta Nipata*, in Andrew Olendzki, *Unlimiting Mind*, Wisdom Publications, Boston 2010, p. 51.
7 *Mahasaccaka Sutta* from the *Majjhima Nikaya*, in *The Middle Length Discourses of the Buddha*, p. 339.
8 *The Dhammapada*, trans. Sangharakshita, Windhorse Publications, Birmingham 2001, p. 58.
9 Analayo, *A Meditator's Life of the Buddha*, Windhorse Publications, Cambridge 2017, p. 202.
10 *Bahiya Sutta* from *The Udana*, in *The Udana and the Itivuttaka*, pp. 19–22.
11 *Culagosinga Sutta* from the *Majjhima Nikaya*, in *The Middle Length Discourses of the Buddha*, pp. 301–6.
12 *Mahagosinga Sutta* from the *Majjhima Nikaya*, in *The Middle Length Discourses of the Buddha*, pp. 308.
13 *Mahagosinga Sutta*, pp. 310–11.
14 *Anapanasati Sutta* from the *Majjhima Nikaya*, in *The Middle*

Length Discourses of the Buddha, pp. 941–8.
15 *Purabheda Sutta* from the *Sutta Nipata*, in *The Sutta-Nipata*, trans. H. Saddhatissa, Curzon, Richmond 1985, pp. 100–1 (slightly modified).
16 *Kosala Sutta* from the *Anguttara Nikaya*, in *The Numerical Discourses of the Buddha*, trans. Bhikkhu Bodhi, Wisdom Publications, Boston 2012, pp. 1383–6.
17 *Pingiya's Praises of the Way to the Beyond* from the *Sutta Nipata*, in *The Sutta-Nipata*, pp. 131–3.
18 *Pingiya's Praises of the Way to the Beyond*, pp. 131–3.
19 *The Numerical Discourses of the Buddha*, p. 147.
20 *The Numerical Discourses of the Buddha*, p. 147.
21 *The Heart as Origami*, ed. Padmacandra, Rising Fire Press, London 2005, pp. 72–3.
22 Tal Ben-Shahar, *Happier*, McGraw-Hill, New York 2007, pp. 65–72.
23 This way of analyzing the conditions that lead to stress first appeared in Dhivan Thomas Jones, *This Being, That Becomes: The Buddha's Teaching on Conditionality*, Windhorse Publications, Cambridge 2011, pp. 23–6.
24 *Bodhi Sutta* (3) from the *Udana*, in *The Udana and the Itivuttaka*, p. 15.
25 *Mahanidana Sutta* from the *Digha Nikaya*, in *The Long Discourses of the Buddha*, trans. Maurice Walshe, Wisdom Publications, Boston 1995, pp. 223–30.
26 *Nibbedhika Sutta* from the *Anguttara Nikaya*, in *The Numerical Discourses of the Buddha*, p. 964.
27 George Eliot, *Middlemarch*, Penguin Books, London 1994, p. 226.
28 Ruth A. Baer, *Practising Happiness*, Robinson, London 2014, pp. 213–14.
29 *Nibbana Sutta* from the *Anguttara Nikaya*, in *The Numerical Discourses of the Buddha*, p. 253.
30 William Blake, 'Eternity', available at https://poets.org/poem/eternity, accessed on 20 January 2023.
31 *Cetana Sutta* from the *Anguttara Nikaya*, in *The Numerical Discourses of the Buddha*, pp. 1554–5.
32 From William Wordsworth, 'Tintern Abbey', available at https://www.bbc.co.uk/poetryseason/poems/tintern_abbey.shtml, accessed on 23 January 2023.
33 *Sappurisadana Sutta* from the *Anguttara Nikaya*, in *The Numerical Discourses of the Buddha*, pp. 763–4.
34 *Abhayarajakumara Sutta* from the *Majjhima Nikaya*, in *The Middle Length Discourses of the Buddha*, pp. 498–501 (simplified).
35 *The Dhammapada*, p. 13.
36 *Dvedhavitakka Sutta* from the *Majjhima Nikaya*, in *The Middle Length Discourses of the Buddha*, pp. 207–10.
37 Paul Gilbert, *The Compassionate Mind*, Constable and Robinson, London 2009, pp. 24–7.

38 Aristotle, *Nicomachean Ethics*, in *The Book of Virtues: A Treasury of Great Moral Stories*, ed. William J. Bennett, Simon & Schuster, New York 1993, p. 101.
39 *The Dhammapada*, p. 49.
40 *Sonadanda Sutta* from the *Digha Nikaya*, in *The Long Discourses of the Buddha*, p. 131.
41 *Upaddha Sutta* from the *Samyutta Nikaya*, in *The Connected Discourses of the Buddha*, trans. Bhikkhu Bodhi, Wisdom Publications, Boston 2000, pp. 1524–5.
42 *The Dhammapada*, p. 14.
43 Sangharakshita, *The Bodhisattva Ideal*, Windhorse Publications, Birmingham 1999, p. 67.
44 *The Heart Sutra*, in *Puja: The Triratna Book of Buddhist Devotional Texts*, Windhorse Publications, Cambridge 2008, p. 24.
45 Robert A.F. Thurman, *The Holy Teaching of Vimalakirti*, Pennsylvania State University Press, Pennsylvania 1976, p. 39.
46 Map by Gunawan Kartapranata - own work combined and redrawn from various sources, CC BY-SA 3.0.
47 Stephen Batchelor, *Verses from the Centre*, Riverhead Books, New York 2000, p. 124.
48 Vasubandhu, *Trimsika* (*Thirty Verses*), available at https://fdocuments.net/document/vasubandhu-trimsika-vasubandhu-trimsika-vijnapti-karika-30-verses.html?page=1, accessed on 20 January 2023.
49 Sangharakshita, 'The essence of Zen', in *The Complete Works of Sangharakshita*, vol. 13: *Eastern and Western Traditions*, Windhorse Publications, Cambridge 2019, p. 333.
50 Ryokan, *One Robe, One Bowl: The Zen Poetry of Ryokan*, trans. John Stevens, Weatherhill, New York and Tokyo 1977, p. 43.
51 Ratnaguna and Sraddhapa, *Great Faith, Great Wisdom*, Windhorse Publications, Cambridge 2016, p. 20.
52 *Surangama Sutra*, in Lama Anagarika Govinda, *Foundations of Tibetan Mysticism*, Weiser, York Beach 1969, p. 256.
53 Sangharakshita, 'Verses of acknowledgement, 1971', in *The Complete Works of Sangharakshita*, vol. 25: *Poems and Short Stories*, Windhorse Publications, Cambridge 2020, p. 331.
54 In the words of Mr Dumby in *Lady Windermere's Fan* (Oscar Wilde, *The Importance of Being Earnest and Other Plays*, Oxford University Press, Oxford 2008, p. 44).
55 *Cetana Sutta*, pp. 1554–5.
56 *Puja: The Triratna Book of Buddhist Devotional Texts*, pp. 36–7.
57 *Puja: The Triratna Book of Buddhist Devotional Texts*, p. 27.
58 *Phena Sutta* from the *Samyutta Nikaya*, in *The Connected Discourses of the Buddha*, pp. 951–3.
59 Kathleen Raine, 'The moment', in *The Collected Poems of Kathleen Raine*, Faber and Faber, London 2019.

60 Vajragupta, *Buddhism: Tools for Living Your Life*, Windhorse Publications, Birmingham 2007.
61 Danapriya, *It's Not Out There*, Windhorse Publications, Cambridge 2020.
62 Vishvapani, *Gautama Buddha: The Life and Teachings of the Awakened One*, Quercus, London 2011.
63 See note 23 above.
64 Paramananda, *Change Your Mind: A Practical Guide to Buddhist Meditation*, Windhorse Publications, Birmingham 1996.
65 Subhadramati, *Not About Being Good: A Practical Guide to Buddhist Ethics*, Windhorse Publications, Cambridge 2013.
66 Nagabodhi, *Sangharakshita: The Boy, the Monk, the Man*, Windhorse Publications, Cambridge 2023.
67 Vessantara, *Meeting the Buddhas*, Windhorse Publications, Cambridge 2022.
68 Prajnaketu, *Cyberloka: A Buddhist Guide to Digital Life*, Windhorse Publications, Cambridge 2022.
69 Vaddhaka Linn, *The Buddha on Wall Street: What's Wrong with Capitalism and What We Can Do About It*, Windhorse Publications, Cambridge 2015.
70 David Loy, *Money, Sex, War, Karma: Notes for a Buddhist Revolution*, Wisdom Publications, Boston 2008.
71 Shantigarbha, *The Burning House: A Buddhist Response to the Climate and Ecological Emergency*, Windhorse Publications, Cambridge 2021.
72 Shantigarbha, *I'll Meet You There: A Practical Guide to Empathy, Mindfulness and Communication*, Windhorse Publications, Cambridge 2018.

Illustration credits

All photographs by Jeremy Peters, except on pages 35, 53, 119, 122, and 130.

All illustrations by Padmacandra, except as noted below.

Page 28 Rupa of emaciated Gautama Buddha by permission of Isabelle Felix and Jayamuni.

Page 30 Rupa of Shakyamuni Buddha with earth touching mudra (at Vajrasana retreat centre) made by Dharmachari Chintamani. By permission of the artist.

Page 33 Rupa of Buddha with teaching mudra by permission of Cambridge Buddhist Centre.

Page 33 Rupa of Buddha lying down by permission of Cambridge Buddhist Centre.

Page 34 Buddha meditating / with meditation mudra by permission of Padmaloka.

Page 35 Figure, Sui dynasty, Hancui, Chonguang Temple by permission of the British Museum

Page 53 Two photographs of a beach by permission of Sagaraghosa.

Page 103 Portrait of Vimalakirti. Sung Dynasty. Unknown Chinese artist. By permission of Alamy.

Page 107 Painting of bamboo by permission of Vimaladipa.

Page 110 Detail of Thousand-Armed Chenresi, a Cosmic Form of the Bodhisattva Avalokiteshvara, the Met, public domain.

Page 113 Photograph by permission of Akshayapradipa and Vimaladipa.

Page 119 Photographs of Sangharakshita by permission of the Urgyen Sangharakshita Trust.

Page 122 Photograph of Sagaraghosa's ordination by permission of Srivati.

Page 130 Photograph of lotus by permission of Sagaraghosa.

Pages 132, 133, 134, 135, 136, 137, 138, 139 All images of the Wheel of Life by permission of Saddharaja.

Page 147 Photograph by permission of Preeti Wathore.
Pages 148, 149 Photographs by permission of Manjunara.
Page 166 *Rouen Cathedral, West Façade, 1894*, Claude Monet, the National Gallery of Art, Washington D.C., Chester Dale Collection, public domain.
Page 166 *Rouen Cathedral, West Façade, Sunlight, 1894*, Claude Monet, the National Gallery of Art, Washington D.C., Chester Dale Collection, public domain.
Page 166 Monet Claude-Oscar (1840–1926) *Cathédrale de Rouen, le portail vue de face, harmonie brune 1892*; © musée d'Orsay/RMN-Grand Palais / Patrice Schmidt /Dist. Photo SCALA, Florence.

Index

Introductory Note

References such as '178-9' indicate (not necessarily continuous) discussion of a topic across a range of pages. Wherever possible in the case of topics with many references, these have either been divided into sub-topics or only the most significant discussions of the topic are listed. Because the entire work is about 'Buddhism' and the 'Buddhist path', the use of these terms (and certain others which occur constantly throughout the book) as an entry point has been restricted. Information will be found under the corresponding detailed topics.

WINDHORSE PUBLICATIONS

Windhorse Publications is a Buddhist charitable company based in the United Kingdom. We place great emphasis on producing books of high quality that are accessible and relevant to those interested in Buddhism at whatever level. We are the main publisher of the works of Sangharakshita, the founder of the Triratna Buddhist Order and Community. Our books draw on the whole range of the Buddhist tradition, including translations of traditional texts, commentaries, books that make links with contemporary culture and ways of life, biographies of Buddhists, and works on meditation.

As a not-for-profit enterprise, we ensure that all surplus income is invested in new books and improved production methods, to better communicate Buddhism in the twenty-first century. We welcome donations to help us continue our work – to find out more, go to windhorsepublications.com.

The Windhorse is a mythical animal that flies over the earth carrying on its back three precious jewels, bringing these invaluable gifts to all humanity: the Buddha (the 'Awakened One'), his teaching, and the community of all his followers.

Windhorse Publications
38 Newmarket Road
Cambridge CB5 8DT
info@windhorsepublications.com

Consortium Book Sales & Distribution
210 American Drive
Jackson TN 38301
USA

Windhorse Books
PO Box 574
Newtown NSW 2042
Australia

THE TRIRATNA BUDDHIST COMMUNITY

Windhorse Publications is a part of the Triratna Buddhist Community, an international movement with centres in Europe, India, North and South America, and Australasia. At these centres, members of the Triratna Buddhist Order offer classes in meditation and Buddhism. Activities of the Triratna Community also include retreat centres, residential spiritual communities, ethical Right Livelihood businesses, and the Karuna Trust, a United Kingdom fundraising charity that supports social welfare projects in the slums and villages of India.

Through these and other activities, Triratna is developing a unique approach to Buddhism, not simply as a philosophy and a set of techniques, but as a creatively directed way of life for all people living in the conditions of the modern world.

If you would like more information about Triratna please visit thebuddhistcentre.com or write to:

London Buddhist Centre
51 Roman Road
London E2 0HU
United Kingdom
contact@lbc.org.uk

Aryaloka
14 Heartwood Circle
Newmarket NH 03857
USA
info@aryaloka.org

Sydney Buddhist Centre
24 Enmore Road
Sydney NSW 2042
Australia
info@sydneybuddhistcentre.org.au